50 Portuguese Pastries Recipes for Home

By: Kelly Johnson

Table of Contents

- Pastéis de Nata (Portuguese Custard Tarts)
- Bola de Berlim (Portuguese Berliner)
- Travesseiros de Sintra (Puff Pastry Pillows from Sintra)
- Queijadas de Sintra (Sintra Cheese Pastries)
- Bolo de Bolacha (Portuguese Biscuit Cake)
- Sonhos (Portuguese Dream Pastries)
- Rabanadas (Portuguese French Toast)
- Pão de Ló (Portuguese Sponge Cake)
- Broas de Mel (Portuguese Honey Cookies)
- Torta de Azeitão (Azeitão Roll Cake)
- Malassadas (Portuguese Fried Dough)
- Papo-Secos (Portuguese Bread Rolls)
- Filhós (Portuguese Fritters)
- Tigeladas (Portuguese Egg Custard Tarts)
- Queijadinhas (Portuguese Cheese Tartlets)
- Ovos Moles de Aveiro (Aveiro Soft Eggs)
- Bolinhos de Amêndoa (Portuguese Almond Cookies)
- Bolo Rei (Portuguese King Cake)
- Fatias Douradas (Portuguese Golden Slices)
- Bolos de Arroz (Portuguese Rice Muffins)
- Pudim Abade de Priscos (Abbot of Priscos Pudding)
- Barrigas de Freira (Nun's Bellies)
- Broa de Avintes (Avintes Cornbread)
- Bolinhos de Coco (Portuguese Coconut Cookies)
- Coscorões (Portuguese Fried Pastry)
- Pão-de-Ló de Margaride (Margaride Sponge Cake)
- Folares (Portuguese Easter Bread)
- Lampreia de Ovos (Portuguese Egg Lamprey)
- Azevias de Grão (Chickpea Turnovers)
- Pão de Ló de Ovar (Ovar Sponge Cake)
- Amêndoas de Cascais (Cascais Almonds)
- Leite Creme (Portuguese Cream)
- Folar de Olhão (Olhão Cake)
- Coscoréis (Portuguese Fried Dough)
- Biscoitos de Azeite (Portuguese Olive Oil Biscuits)
- Pão de Rala (Portuguese Bread of Rala)

- Bolo de Noz (Portuguese Walnut Cake)
- Doce Fino (Portuguese Fine Pastry)
- Biscoitos de Aguardente (Portuguese Brandy Biscuits)
- Azevias de Batata Doce (Sweet Potato Turnovers)
- Bolo de Maçã (Portuguese Apple Cake)
- Pinhões (Portuguese Pine Nut Cookies)
- Pão de Deus (Portuguese Bread of God)
- Charutos de Ovos (Portuguese Egg Cigars)
- Pão de Rala (Portuguese Bread of Rala)
- Bolo de Cenoura (Portuguese Carrot Cake)
- Pastel de Chaves (Chaves Pastry)
- Castanhas de Ovos (Portuguese Chestnuts of Eggs)
- Coscorões (Portuguese Fried Pastry)
- Pão de Ló de Alfeizerão (Alfeizerão Sponge Cake)

Pastéis de Nata (Portuguese Custard Tarts)

Ingredients:

- **Pastry:**
    - Puff pastry sheets (store-bought or homemade)
    - Flour (for dusting)
- **Custard Filling:**
    - 2 cups (500 ml) whole milk
    - 1 cinnamon stick
    - Peel of 1/2 lemon (optional)
    - 6 large egg yolks
    - 1/2 cup (100 g) granulated sugar
    - 2 tbsp all-purpose flour
    - 2 tbsp cornstarch
- **Sugar Topping:**
    - Granulated sugar for sprinkling

Instructions:

1. **Prepare the Custard:**
    - In a saucepan, combine the milk, cinnamon stick, and lemon peel (if using). Heat over medium heat until just simmering. Remove from heat and let it infuse for about 15 minutes. Strain the milk mixture and discard the cinnamon stick and lemon peel.
2. **Make the Custard Base:**
    - In a bowl, whisk together the egg yolks, sugar, flour, and cornstarch until smooth and pale yellow.
    - Slowly pour the infused milk into the egg mixture, whisking continuously to prevent curdling.
3. **Cook the Custard:**
    - Pour the mixture back into the saucepan and cook over medium heat, stirring constantly with a wooden spoon or whisk. Cook until the mixture thickens to a custard consistency that coats the back of a spoon, about 5-7 minutes. It should be smooth and without lumps.
    - Remove from heat and transfer the custard to a bowl. Cover with plastic wrap directly touching the surface of the custard to prevent a skin from forming. Let it cool to room temperature, then refrigerate for at least 1 hour (or overnight) to chill completely.
4. **Prepare the Pastry:**
    - Preheat your oven to 475°F (245°C).
    - Roll out the puff pastry on a lightly floured surface into a large rectangle, about 1/8 inch (3 mm) thick.

- Starting from one short end, tightly roll up the pastry like a jelly roll. Cut the roll into 12 equal pieces.

5. **Form the Pastéis de Nata:**
   - Take each piece of pastry and place it cut-side down. Flatten with the palm of your hand, then use a rolling pin to roll out into a thin circle, about 4 inches (10 cm) in diameter.
   - Press each circle into the cups of a standard muffin tin, pressing the dough up the sides to form a pastry shell.

6. **Fill and Bake:**
   - Fill each pastry shell with the chilled custard, filling each about 3/4 full.
   - Sprinkle the tops of each tart with a little granulated sugar.
   - Bake in the preheated oven for about 10-12 minutes, or until the pastry is golden brown and the tops are blistered and caramelized.

7. **Cool and Serve:**
   - Remove the pastéis de nata from the oven and let them cool in the tin for a few minutes.
   - Carefully remove the tarts from the tin and transfer to a wire rack to cool completely.
   - Enjoy warm or at room temperature, dusted with powdered sugar and cinnamon if desired.

Tips:

- For an authentic touch, use a blowtorch to caramelize the sugar on top after baking.
- Pastéis de Nata are best served fresh but can be stored in an airtight container in the refrigerator for up to 3 days.

These Portuguese Custard Tarts are a delightful combination of flaky pastry and creamy custard, sure to impress anyone who tries them!

Bola de Berlim (Portuguese Berliner)

Ingredients:

For the Dough:

- 500g all-purpose flour
- 75g granulated sugar
- 10g active dry yeast
- 200ml lukewarm milk
- 2 large eggs
- 75g unsalted butter, softened
- Pinch of salt
- Zest of 1 lemon or orange (optional)
- Vegetable oil, for frying

For the Filling:

- Custard or jam of your choice (traditionally custard)

For Dusting:

- Powdered sugar

Instructions:

1. **Prepare the Dough:**
    - In a small bowl, dissolve the yeast in lukewarm milk with a pinch of sugar. Let it sit for about 5-10 minutes until frothy.
    - In a large mixing bowl or the bowl of a stand mixer fitted with a dough hook, combine the flour, sugar, and salt. Make a well in the center.
    - Add the frothy yeast mixture, eggs, softened butter, and lemon or orange zest (if using) to the flour mixture. Mix until a soft dough forms.
    - Knead the dough for about 8-10 minutes by hand on a floured surface, or 5-7 minutes using a stand mixer on medium speed, until the dough is smooth and elastic.
    - Place the dough in a lightly greased bowl, cover with a clean kitchen towel or plastic wrap, and let it rise in a warm place for about 1-2 hours, or until doubled in size.
2. **Shape and Fry the Bolas de Berlim:**
    - Once the dough has risen, punch it down to release the air. Divide the dough into equal-sized pieces (about 60-70g each) and shape each piece into a smooth ball.
    - Place the dough balls on a lightly floured surface, cover with a clean kitchen towel, and let them rest for about 15-20 minutes.
    - In a deep, heavy-bottomed pot or fryer, heat vegetable oil to 350°F (175°C).

- Carefully place a few dough balls at a time into the hot oil, making sure not to overcrowd the pot. Fry for about 2-3 minutes on each side, or until they are golden brown and cooked through.
- Remove the fried dough balls with a slotted spoon and drain them on paper towels to remove excess oil. Let them cool slightly.

3. **Fill the Bolas de Berlim:**
    - Once the fried dough balls are cool enough to handle but still warm, use a piping bag fitted with a small tip to inject custard or jam into each ball. Insert the tip into the side of the ball and gently squeeze until the ball feels slightly heavier and the filling starts to ooze out.
4. **Dust and Serve:**
    - Dust the filled Bolas de Berlim generously with powdered sugar.
    - Serve warm or at room temperature. They are best enjoyed fresh on the day they are made.

Tips:

- Ensure the oil is at the right temperature (around 350°F or 175°C) to fry the Bolas de Berlim properly and achieve a golden-brown color.
- If using custard, make sure it is thick enough to hold its shape but still creamy and smooth.
- You can vary the filling by using different types of jams or even chocolate ganache for a different twist.

Bola de Berlim are a delightful Portuguese treat, perfect for enjoying with a cup of coffee or tea, and they are sure to satisfy your sweet tooth!

Travesseiros de Sintra (Puff Pastry Pillows from Sintra)

Ingredients:

For the Almond Cream Filling:

- 200g almond meal or finely ground almonds
- 200g granulated sugar
- 50g unsalted butter, softened
- 2 large egg yolks
- Zest of 1 lemon
- 1 tbsp all-purpose flour

For the Assembly:

- 1 package (about 400g) of store-bought puff pastry sheets (or homemade)
- Powdered sugar, for dusting

Instructions:

1. **Prepare the Almond Cream Filling:**
   - In a bowl, combine the almond meal, granulated sugar, softened butter, egg yolks, lemon zest, and flour. Mix until smooth and well combined. The mixture should be thick and spreadable. Set aside.
2. **Prepare the Puff Pastry:**
   - If using store-bought puff pastry sheets, follow the package instructions for thawing, if frozen.
   - On a lightly floured surface, roll out the puff pastry sheets into a rectangle about 1/8 inch (3 mm) thick.
3. **Assemble the Travesseiros de Sintra:**
   - Spread the almond cream filling evenly over one half of the rolled-out puff pastry sheet, leaving a border around the edges.
   - Fold the other half of the pastry sheet over the filling to cover it completely, creating a large filled rectangle.
4. **Cut and Shape:**
   - Use a sharp knife or pastry cutter to trim the edges of the rectangle to create a neat shape.
   - Cut the filled pastry into smaller rectangles or squares, about 2-3 inches (5-7 cm) wide and 4-5 inches (10-12 cm) long.
5. **Bake:**
   - Preheat your oven to 375°F (190°C).
   - Place the filled pastry pillows on a baking sheet lined with parchment paper, leaving some space between each one.
   - Bake in the preheated oven for about 20-25 minutes, or until the pastry is golden brown and puffed up.
6. **Finish:**

- Remove the Travesseiros de Sintra from the oven and let them cool slightly on a wire rack.
- Dust generously with powdered sugar before serving.

Tips:

- Ensure that the almond cream filling is not too runny to prevent it from leaking out during baking.
- You can enhance the flavor by adding a pinch of cinnamon or a splash of almond extract to the filling.
- Travesseiros de Sintra are best enjoyed fresh on the day they are made but can be stored in an airtight container for a day or two.

These Travesseiros de Sintra are a delightful combination of crispy puff pastry and sweet almond cream filling, capturing the essence of Portuguese pastry craftsmanship. Enjoy these treats with a cup of coffee or tea for a truly indulgent experience!

Queijadas de Sintra (Sintra Cheese Pastries)

Ingredients:

For the Pastry Dough:

- 250g all-purpose flour
- 100g unsalted butter, cold and cut into cubes
- 1/4 tsp salt
- 1/4 cup (50g) granulated sugar
- 1 large egg
- Cold water, as needed

For the Cheese Filling:

- 250g fresh cheese (Portuguese queijo fresco or a mix of ricotta and cream cheese)
- 100g granulated sugar
- 2 large eggs
- Zest of 1 lemon
- 1 tbsp all-purpose flour
- Powdered sugar, for dusting

Instructions:

1. **Prepare the Pastry Dough:**
    - In a large bowl, combine the flour, salt, and granulated sugar.
    - Add the cold butter cubes and rub them into the flour mixture using your fingertips until it resembles coarse breadcrumbs.
    - Add the egg and mix until the dough starts to come together. If needed, add a little cold water, a teaspoon at a time, until the dough forms a ball.
    - Wrap the dough in plastic wrap and refrigerate for at least 30 minutes to firm up.
2. **Make the Cheese Filling:**
    - In a mixing bowl, combine the fresh cheese, granulated sugar, eggs, lemon zest, and flour. Mix until smooth and well combined. The mixture should be creamy and slightly thick.
3. **Assemble the Queijadas de Sintra:**
    - Preheat your oven to 375°F (190°C). Lightly grease a muffin tin or line it with paper liners.
    - On a lightly floured surface, roll out the chilled pastry dough to about 1/8 inch (3 mm) thick. Using a round cookie cutter or a glass, cut out circles slightly larger than the size of your muffin tin cups.
    - Gently press each circle of pastry dough into the prepared muffin tin cups, making sure to press the dough up the sides.
    - Spoon the cheese filling evenly into each pastry shell, filling each about 3/4 full.
4. **Bake:**

- Bake the queijadas in the preheated oven for about 20-25 minutes, or until the pastry is golden brown and the filling is set. The tops may crack slightly, which is normal.

5. **Cool and Serve:**
   - Remove the queijadas from the oven and let them cool in the muffin tin for a few minutes.
   - Carefully remove the queijadas from the muffin tin and transfer them to a wire rack to cool completely.
   - Dust with powdered sugar before serving, if desired.

Tips:

- If you cannot find Portuguese queijo fresco, you can use a mix of ricotta and cream cheese for a similar texture and flavor.
- Queijadas de Sintra are traditionally served at room temperature or slightly warm. They can be stored in an airtight container in the refrigerator for a few days.
- The lemon zest adds a refreshing citrus note to the filling, but you can omit it if you prefer a more straightforward cheese flavor.

Enjoy these Queijadas de Sintra as a delightful taste of Portuguese pastry craftsmanship, perfect for any occasion or as a sweet treat with coffee or tea!

Bolo de Bolacha (Portuguese Biscuit Cake)

Ingredients:

For the Cake:

- 1 package (about 200g) of Maria biscuits or similar tea biscuits
- Strong brewed coffee, cooled (enough to soak the biscuits)

For the Cream Filling:

- 200g unsalted butter, softened
- 1 can (397g) sweetened condensed milk
- 1 tsp vanilla extract

For Garnish (optional):

- Cocoa powder or grated chocolate for dusting

Instructions:

1. **Prepare the Cream Filling:**
   - In a mixing bowl, beat the softened butter until creamy and smooth.
   - Gradually add the sweetened condensed milk, continuing to beat until well combined and fluffy.
   - Add the vanilla extract and mix until incorporated. Set aside.
2. **Assemble the Bolo de Bolacha:**
   - Dip each biscuit into the cooled brewed coffee, one at a time, ensuring they are well soaked but not overly soggy.
   - Arrange a layer of soaked biscuits on a serving plate or cake stand, placing them side by side to form a solid base.
   - Spread a generous layer of the cream filling evenly over the layer of biscuits.
   - Repeat the layers: dip more biscuits in coffee, arrange them on top of the cream filling in a single layer, and then spread another layer of cream filling on top.
   - Continue alternating layers of soaked biscuits and cream filling until you use up all the biscuits and filling, ending with a layer of cream on top.
3. **Chill and Garnish:**
   - Cover the assembled Bolo de Bolacha with plastic wrap and refrigerate for at least 4 hours, or preferably overnight. Chilling helps the flavors meld and the biscuits soften to a cake-like texture.
   - Before serving, dust the top of the cake with cocoa powder or grated chocolate for decoration.

Tips:

- Make sure the coffee is completely cooled before soaking the biscuits to prevent them from becoming too soggy.
- You can adjust the sweetness of the cream filling by adding more or less condensed milk, depending on your preference.
- Bolo de Bolacha is best served chilled. It can be stored in the refrigerator for several days, covered, but the biscuits will continue to soften over time.

This Bolo de Bolacha is a simple yet delicious dessert that is popular in Portugal, enjoyed for its creamy texture and coffee-infused biscuit layers. It's perfect for gatherings or as a sweet treat with afternoon tea or coffee. Enjoy!

Sonhos (Portuguese Dream Pastries)

Ingredients:

- 1 cup (240 ml) water
- 1/4 cup (60 ml) unsalted butter
- Pinch of salt
- 1 cup (125 g) all-purpose flour
- 4 large eggs
- Vegetable oil, for frying
- Granulated sugar and ground cinnamon, for dusting

Instructions:

1. **Prepare the Dough:**
    - In a medium saucepan, bring the water, butter, and salt to a boil over medium heat.
    - Reduce the heat to low and add the flour all at once, stirring vigorously with a wooden spoon until the mixture forms a smooth dough and pulls away from the sides of the pan. This should take about 1-2 minutes.
    - Remove the pan from the heat and let the dough cool slightly, about 5 minutes.
2. **Add Eggs:**
    - Add the eggs, one at a time, to the dough, beating well after each addition. The dough will be sticky and smooth.
3. **Shape and Fry:**
    - Heat vegetable oil in a deep, heavy-bottomed pot or fryer to 350°F (175°C).
    - Using two spoons or a small ice cream scoop, drop spoonfuls of dough into the hot oil, working in batches to avoid overcrowding.
    - Fry the sonhos for about 5-7 minutes, turning occasionally with a slotted spoon, until they are golden brown and cooked through.
4. **Drain and Dust:**
    - Remove the fried sonhos from the oil using a slotted spoon and drain them on paper towels to remove excess oil.
    - While still warm, roll the sonhos in a mixture of granulated sugar and ground cinnamon until evenly coated.
5. **Serve:**
    - Serve the sonhos warm or at room temperature. They are best enjoyed fresh on the day they are made.

Tips:

- The dough should be at a consistency where it holds its shape but is still soft enough to pipe or drop easily into the hot oil.

- Make sure the oil is at the right temperature (around 350°F or 175°C) to fry the sonhos evenly and achieve a golden-brown color.
- You can customize the flavor by adding a hint of lemon zest or a splash of vanilla extract to the dough.

Sonhos are a delightful treat, crispy on the outside and airy on the inside, perfect for celebrating special occasions or enjoying as a sweet indulgence with family and friends.

Rabanadas (Portuguese French Toast)

Ingredients:

- 1 loaf of day-old bread (traditionally Portuguese bread like Bolo do Caco, but any sturdy bread like French or Italian bread will work)
- 2 cups (480 ml) milk
- 4 large eggs
- 1/2 cup (100 g) granulated sugar
- 1 cinnamon stick (or 1 tsp ground cinnamon)
- Zest of 1 lemon (optional)
- Pinch of salt
- Vegetable oil, for frying
- Granulated sugar and ground cinnamon, for dusting

Instructions:

1. **Prepare the Bread:**
   - Slice the day-old bread into thick slices, about 1-inch (2.5 cm) thick. You can trim off the crusts if desired, although it's not necessary.
2. **Prepare the Milk Mixture:**
   - In a saucepan, combine the milk, cinnamon stick (if using), lemon zest (if using), and a pinch of salt. Heat over medium heat until just simmering. Remove from heat and let it cool slightly.
3. **Soak the Bread:**
   - In a shallow dish or bowl, whisk the eggs and granulated sugar until well combined.
   - Dip each slice of bread into the milk mixture, ensuring it is soaked on both sides but not overly saturated.
4. **Fry the Rabanadas:**
   - Heat vegetable oil in a large skillet or frying pan over medium-high heat.
   - Carefully place the soaked bread slices in the hot oil and fry until golden brown and crispy on both sides, about 2-3 minutes per side.
   - Remove the fried Rabanadas from the oil and drain them on paper towels to remove excess oil.
5. **Dust and Serve:**
   - While still warm, sprinkle the Rabanadas with a mixture of granulated sugar and ground cinnamon, ensuring they are evenly coated.
   - Serve Rabanadas warm or at room temperature. They can be enjoyed on their own or with a sprinkle of powdered sugar on top.

Tips:

- Adjust the sweetness by adding more or less sugar to the egg mixture or the sugar-cinnamon coating.
- You can enhance the flavor by adding a splash of vanilla extract or a pinch of nutmeg to the egg mixture.
- Rabanadas are best served fresh, but you can store any leftovers in an airtight container in the refrigerator and reheat them gently in the oven before serving.

Enjoy these Rabanadas as a delightful Portuguese treat, perfect for breakfast, dessert, or as a snack with a cup of coffee or tea!

Pão de Ló (Portuguese Sponge Cake)

Ingredients:

- 6 large eggs, at room temperature
- 1 cup (200g) granulated sugar
- 1 cup (120g) cake flour (or all-purpose flour, sifted)
- 1/2 tsp vanilla extract
- Pinch of salt

Instructions:

1. **Preheat the Oven and Prepare the Pan:**
    - Preheat your oven to 350°F (180°C). Grease and flour a 9-inch (23 cm) round cake pan, tapping out any excess flour.
2. **Prepare the Eggs:**
    - In a large mixing bowl, crack the eggs and add the granulated sugar and a pinch of salt.
3. **Beat the Eggs and Sugar:**
    - Using an electric mixer or a stand mixer fitted with the whisk attachment, beat the eggs and sugar on high speed until pale, fluffy, and tripled in volume. This will take about 8-10 minutes. The mixture should form ribbons when you lift the beaters.
4. **Fold in the Flour:**
    - Sift the cake flour (or all-purpose flour) over the beaten egg mixture in two or three additions, gently folding it in with a spatula after each addition. Be careful not to deflate the batter too much.
5. **Add Vanilla Extract:**
    - Gently fold in the vanilla extract until just incorporated.
6. **Bake the Pão de Ló:**
    - Pour the batter into the prepared cake pan and smooth the top with a spatula.
    - Bake in the preheated oven for 25-30 minutes, or until the top is golden brown and a toothpick inserted into the center comes out clean or with a few crumbs attached.
7. **Cooling:**
    - Remove the cake from the oven and let it cool in the pan for about 10 minutes.
    - Carefully run a knife around the edges of the cake to loosen it from the pan, then transfer it to a wire rack to cool completely.
8. **Serve:**
    - Once cooled, slice and serve the Pão de Ló on its own or with a dusting of powdered sugar. It's also delicious served with fresh berries or a dollop of whipped cream.

Tips:

- For best results, use room temperature eggs and beat them until they are very fluffy and pale. This helps create a light and airy texture in the cake.
- Be gentle when folding in the flour to avoid overmixing, which can result in a dense cake.
- Pão de Ló can be stored in an airtight container at room temperature for up to 3 days, or it can be frozen for longer storage.

Enjoy this classic Portuguese Pão de Ló as a delightful dessert or tea-time treat, showcasing the simplicity and elegance of Portuguese baking tradition!

Broas de Mel (Portuguese Honey Cookies)

Ingredients:

- 2 cups (250g) all-purpose flour
- 1 cup (200g) granulated sugar
- 1/2 cup (120ml) honey
- 1/4 cup (60ml) olive oil (or vegetable oil)
- 1 tsp ground cinnamon
- 1/2 tsp ground cloves
- Zest of 1 lemon
- 1 tsp baking soda
- Pinch of salt
- Additional flour for dusting

Instructions:

1. **Prepare the Dough:**
    - In a large mixing bowl, combine the flour, sugar, ground cinnamon, ground cloves, lemon zest, baking soda, and a pinch of salt. Mix well to combine.
    - In a small saucepan, heat the honey and olive oil over low heat until warmed and well combined. Remove from heat and let it cool slightly.
    - Pour the warm honey mixture into the dry ingredients and mix until a smooth dough forms. The dough will be slightly sticky but should hold together.
2. **Shape the Cookies:**
    - Preheat your oven to 350°F (175°C). Line a baking sheet with parchment paper.
    - Lightly dust your hands and the work surface with flour. Take small portions of the dough and roll them into balls about 1 inch (2.5 cm) in diameter. Place them on the prepared baking sheet, spacing them a few inches apart.
3. **Bake the Broas:**
    - Bake in the preheated oven for 10-12 minutes, or until the cookies are lightly golden brown and set.
4. **Cool and Serve:**
    - Remove the cookies from the oven and let them cool on the baking sheet for a few minutes before transferring them to a wire rack to cool completely.
    - Once cooled, store the Broas de Mel in an airtight container at room temperature. They can be enjoyed for several days.

Tips:

- The dough may be slightly sticky, so dusting your hands and work surface with flour will make it easier to handle.
- Feel free to adjust the spices according to your taste. Some recipes also include ground ginger or nutmeg for additional flavor.

- Broas de Mel are traditionally enjoyed with a cup of coffee or tea, or as a sweet treat during festive gatherings.

These Broas de Mel capture the essence of Portuguese baking with their rich honey flavor and warm spices, making them a perfect addition to your holiday baking repertoire. Enjoy these cookies as a delightful taste of Portuguese culinary tradition!

Torta de Azeitão (Azeitão Roll Cake)

Ingredients:

For the Cake:

- 6 large eggs, separated
- 150g granulated sugar
- 100g cake flour (or all-purpose flour)
- 1/2 tsp vanilla extract
- Zest of 1 lemon
- Pinch of salt

For the Filling:

- 6 large egg yolks
- 200g granulated sugar
- 200ml water
- Zest of 1 lemon
- 1 tbsp cornstarch
- 200ml heavy cream

Additional:

- Powdered sugar, for dusting

Instructions:

1. **Prepare the Cake:**
   - Preheat your oven to 350°F (180°C). Grease a 13x9 inch (33x23 cm) baking pan and line it with parchment paper.
   - In a large mixing bowl, beat the egg yolks with half of the granulated sugar (75g) until pale and fluffy. Add the vanilla extract and lemon zest, and mix until combined.
   - In a separate bowl, beat the egg whites with a pinch of salt until soft peaks form. Gradually add the remaining granulated sugar (75g) and continue beating until stiff peaks form.
   - Gently fold the beaten egg whites into the egg yolk mixture, a third at a time, using a spatula.
   - Sift the flour over the batter in two or three additions, gently folding it in until fully incorporated and no lumps remain.
   - Pour the batter into the prepared baking pan, spreading it evenly with a spatula.
   - Bake in the preheated oven for 12-15 minutes, or until the cake is golden brown and springs back when lightly touched.
2. **Make the Filling:**

- In a saucepan, combine the granulated sugar, water, lemon zest, and cornstarch. Cook over medium heat, stirring constantly, until the mixture thickens and boils.
- In a bowl, whisk the egg yolks. Gradually pour the hot sugar mixture into the egg yolks, whisking constantly.
- Return the mixture to the saucepan and cook over low heat, stirring constantly, until it thickens to a custard consistency. Remove from heat and let it cool completely.
- In a separate bowl, whip the heavy cream until stiff peaks form. Gently fold the whipped cream into the cooled custard mixture until well combined.

3. **Assemble the Roll Cake:**
    - Once the cake has cooled slightly, but is still warm, carefully flip it onto a clean kitchen towel dusted with powdered sugar.
    - Peel off the parchment paper from the cake.
    - Spread the custard filling evenly over the entire surface of the cake.
    - Starting from one short end, use the towel to help roll the cake into a tight spiral. Transfer the rolled cake to a serving platter with the seam side down.

4. **Chill and Serve:**
    - Chill the Torta de Azeitão in the refrigerator for at least 1 hour before serving to set the filling.
    - Before serving, dust the top of the roll cake with powdered sugar for decoration.

Tips:

- Be gentle when folding the egg whites into the batter to keep the cake light and fluffy.
- Ensure the custard filling is completely cooled before mixing in the whipped cream to maintain its creamy texture.
- You can customize the flavor by adding a splash of Port wine or a sprinkle of cinnamon to the custard filling for a traditional touch.

Torta de Azeitão is a delightful Portuguese dessert, perfect for special occasions or as a sweet treat with coffee or tea. Enjoy this roll cake with its creamy custard filling and light sponge cake exterior, capturing the essence of Portuguese culinary heritage!

Malassadas (Portuguese Fried Dough)

Ingredients:

- 4 cups (500g) all-purpose flour
- 1/2 cup (100g) granulated sugar
- 1 tsp salt
- 1 tsp ground cinnamon (optional)
- 2 tsp instant yeast
- 1 cup (240ml) lukewarm milk
- 4 large eggs
- 1/4 cup (60g) unsalted butter, melted
- Vegetable oil, for frying
- Powdered sugar, for dusting

Instructions:

1. **Prepare the Dough:**
    - In a large mixing bowl, combine the flour, sugar, salt, ground cinnamon (if using), and instant yeast.
    - In a separate bowl, whisk together the lukewarm milk, eggs, and melted butter.
    - Gradually pour the wet ingredients into the dry ingredients, stirring with a wooden spoon or using a stand mixer with a dough hook attachment, until a smooth dough forms. The dough should be soft and slightly sticky.
    - Cover the bowl with plastic wrap or a clean kitchen towel and let the dough rise in a warm place until doubled in size, about 1-2 hours.
2. **Shape and Fry the Malassadas:**
    - Heat vegetable oil in a deep, heavy-bottomed pot or fryer to 350°F (175°C).
    - Lightly flour your hands and pinch off pieces of dough (about 2-3 tablespoons each) to form balls. Roll each piece of dough into a smooth ball and place it on a baking sheet lined with parchment paper.
    - Carefully place a few dough balls into the hot oil, being careful not to overcrowd the pot. Fry them for about 3-4 minutes, turning occasionally with a slotted spoon, until they are golden brown and cooked through.
3. **Drain and Dust:**
    - Remove the fried Malassadas from the oil using a slotted spoon and drain them on paper towels to remove excess oil.
    - While still warm, dust the Malassadas generously with powdered sugar. You can also roll them in cinnamon sugar if desired.
4. **Serve:**
    - Serve the Malassadas warm or at room temperature. They are best enjoyed fresh on the day they are made.

Tips:

- Ensure the oil is at the correct temperature (around 350°F or 175°C) to fry the Malassadas evenly and achieve a crispy exterior.
- You can flavor the dough with lemon or orange zest for a citrusy twist, or add a splash of vanilla extract or rum for extra flavor.
- Malassadas are often enjoyed as they are, but you can also serve them with a dipping sauce like chocolate ganache or dulce de leche for a decadent treat.

Enjoy these Portuguese Malassadas as a delightful and festive treat, perfect for celebrating special occasions or simply indulging in a sweet snack!

Papo-Secos (Portuguese Bread Rolls)

Ingredients:

- 500g (4 cups) bread flour
- 10g (2 tsp) instant yeast
- 10g (2 tsp) salt
- 300ml (1 1/4 cups) lukewarm water
- 30ml (2 tbsp) olive oil
- 1 tbsp granulated sugar
- Cornmeal or semolina flour, for dusting (optional)
- Egg wash (1 egg beaten with a tablespoon of water), for brushing (optional)

Instructions:

1. **Mixing the Dough:**
    - In a large mixing bowl or the bowl of a stand mixer fitted with a dough hook, combine the bread flour, instant yeast, salt, and sugar.
    - Make a well in the center and add the lukewarm water and olive oil.
    - Mix the ingredients together until a rough dough forms.
2. **Kneading:**
    - Knead the dough for about 10-15 minutes by hand on a lightly floured surface or with the dough hook attachment on medium speed, until the dough is smooth, elastic, and no longer sticky.
3. **First Rise:**
    - Place the dough in a lightly oiled bowl, cover with plastic wrap or a clean kitchen towel, and let it rise in a warm place for about 1-2 hours, or until doubled in size.
4. **Shaping:**
    - Once doubled in size, gently deflate the dough and divide it into equal-sized portions (usually 8-10 pieces).
    - Shape each portion into a round ball by folding the edges towards the center and pinching them together underneath.
5. **Second Rise:**
    - Place the shaped rolls on a baking sheet lined with parchment paper, leaving some space between them.
    - Cover the rolls loosely with plastic wrap or a kitchen towel and let them rise again for about 30-45 minutes, until they have puffed up and almost doubled in size.
6. **Baking:**
    - Preheat your oven to 400°F (200°C) during the last 15 minutes of the second rise.
    - If using, lightly dust the tops of the rolls with cornmeal or semolina flour for a rustic crust.
    - Optionally, brush the rolls with egg wash for a shiny finish.

- Bake the rolls in the preheated oven for 15-20 minutes, or until they are golden brown and sound hollow when tapped on the bottom.
7. **Cooling:**
    - Remove the rolls from the oven and transfer them to a wire rack to cool completely.
8. **Serve:**
    - Serve Papo-Secos fresh on the day they are made. They are delicious served warm with butter, cheese, cold cuts, or any of your favorite sandwich fillings.

Tips:

- For a more authentic touch, you can sprinkle the rolls with a little water just before baking to create a slightly crispier crust.
- If you prefer smaller or larger rolls, adjust the size accordingly and monitor the baking time accordingly.
- Store any leftover rolls in an airtight container once they have cooled completely. They can be reheated in a toaster oven for a few minutes before serving to regain their freshness.

Enjoy these homemade Papo-Secos as a versatile addition to your meals, whether for breakfast, sandwiches, or as a side to soups and stews. They embody the delicious simplicity of Portuguese bread-making tradition!

Filhós (Portuguese Fritters)

Ingredients:

- 2 cups (250g) all-purpose flour
- 2 tbsp granulated sugar
- 1/2 tsp salt
- 1/2 tsp ground cinnamon (optional)
- 2 large eggs
- 1 cup (240ml) milk
- Zest of 1 lemon or orange
- 1/2 tsp vanilla extract
- Vegetable oil, for frying
- Powdered sugar, for dusting

Instructions:

1. **Mixing the Dough:**
    - In a large mixing bowl, whisk together the flour, sugar, salt, and ground cinnamon (if using).
    - In a separate bowl, whisk together the eggs, milk, lemon or orange zest, and vanilla extract.
    - Gradually add the wet ingredients to the dry ingredients, whisking until a smooth batter forms. The batter should be thick but pourable.
2. **Resting the Batter:**
    - Cover the bowl with plastic wrap or a clean kitchen towel and let the batter rest at room temperature for about 30 minutes to 1 hour. This helps the gluten relax and allows the flavors to meld.
3. **Frying the Filhós:**
    - Heat vegetable oil in a deep, heavy-bottomed pot or fryer to 350°F (175°C).
    - Using a spoon or your hands, carefully drop portions of the batter into the hot oil, shaping them into round or irregular shapes. You can make them small or large, depending on your preference.
    - Fry the Filhós in batches, turning occasionally with a slotted spoon, until they are golden brown and cooked through, about 2-3 minutes per side.
4. **Draining and Dusting:**
    - Remove the fried Filhós from the oil with a slotted spoon and drain them on paper towels to remove excess oil.
    - While still warm, dust the Filhós generously with powdered sugar.
5. **Serve:**
    - Serve the Filhós warm or at room temperature. They are best enjoyed fresh on the day they are made.

Tips:

- Be cautious when frying the Filhós to ensure they cook evenly and don't brown too quickly.
- You can vary the flavor by adding a pinch of nutmeg or cardamom to the batter for a spiced variation.
- Filhós are a festive treat that can be enjoyed on their own or with a cup of coffee or tea.

These sweet Filhós capture the essence of Portuguese culinary tradition with their crispy exterior and tender interior, making them a delightful treat for special occasions or any time you crave something sweet and comforting.

Tigeladas (Portuguese Egg Custard Tarts)

Ingredients:

- 6 large eggs
- 1 cup (200g) granulated sugar
- 1/2 cup (60g) all-purpose flour
- 4 cups (1 liter) milk
- Zest of 1 lemon
- Butter or oil, for greasing

Instructions:

1. **Preheat the Oven:**
    - Preheat your oven to 350°F (175°C). Grease individual ramekins or a baking dish with butter or oil.
2. **Prepare the Batter:**
    - In a large mixing bowl, whisk together the eggs and granulated sugar until well combined.
    - Gradually whisk in the flour until smooth and no lumps remain.
    - Heat the milk in a saucepan over medium heat until it just begins to simmer. Remove from heat.
    - Slowly pour the hot milk into the egg mixture, whisking constantly, to temper the eggs and avoid scrambling them.
    - Stir in the lemon zest to flavor the custard.
3. **Bake the Tigeladas:**
    - Pour the custard mixture into the prepared ramekins or baking dish.
    - Place the ramekins or baking dish in a larger roasting pan or baking dish. Fill the larger dish with hot water halfway up the sides of the ramekins (this creates a water bath or bain-marie).
    - Carefully transfer the water bath to the preheated oven and bake for about 45-50 minutes, or until the custard is set and lightly golden on top. The edges should be slightly firm and the center still slightly jiggly.
4. **Cooling and Serving:**
    - Remove the Tigeladas from the oven and let them cool slightly in the water bath.
    - Serve the Tigeladas warm or at room temperature. They can be enjoyed on their own or dusted with powdered sugar or cinnamon for extra flavor.

Tips:

- Tigeladas are traditionally baked in individual ceramic ramekins, but you can also use a larger baking dish and cut them into squares for serving.
- The lemon zest adds a bright flavor to the custard, but you can also experiment with vanilla extract or cinnamon for different variations.

- Make sure not to overbake the Tigeladas; they should have a creamy, custard-like texture when done.

Enjoy these delicious Tigeladas as a delightful Portuguese dessert, perfect for any occasion or as a sweet treat with a cup of coffee or tea!

Queijadinhas (Portuguese Cheese Tartlets)

Ingredients:

- 250g (about 1 cup) fresh cheese (such as ricotta or queijo fresco), well drained
- 3/4 cup (150g) granulated sugar
- 3 large eggs
- Zest of 1 lemon
- 1/4 cup (60ml) milk
- 2 tbsp all-purpose flour
- Butter or oil, for greasing muffin tin

Instructions:

1. **Preheat the Oven:**
   - Preheat your oven to 350°F (175°C). Grease a muffin tin with butter or oil.
2. **Prepare the Batter:**
   - In a large mixing bowl, combine the fresh cheese and granulated sugar. Mix well until smooth and creamy.
   - Add the eggs, one at a time, mixing well after each addition.
   - Stir in the lemon zest and milk until well combined.
   - Gradually add the flour, mixing until the batter is smooth and no lumps remain.
3. **Fill the Muffin Tin:**
   - Pour the batter into the prepared muffin tin, filling each cavity about 3/4 full.
4. **Bake the Queijadinhas:**
   - Bake in the preheated oven for 20-25 minutes, or until the tartlets are set and lightly golden on top. They should puff up slightly.
5. **Cooling and Serving:**
   - Remove the Queijadinhas from the oven and let them cool in the muffin tin for a few minutes.
   - Carefully remove them from the muffin tin and transfer to a wire rack to cool completely.
6. **Serve:**
   - Serve the Queijadinhas at room temperature. They can be enjoyed on their own or dusted with powdered sugar for extra sweetness.

Tips:

- You can add a splash of vanilla extract or a pinch of cinnamon to the batter for additional flavor.
- Make sure the fresh cheese is well drained to avoid excess moisture in the tartlets.
- Queijadinhas can be stored in an airtight container in the refrigerator for a few days. Enjoy them cold or reheat them gently in the oven before serving.

These Queijadinhas are a wonderful example of Portuguese pastry tradition, offering a creamy, cheesy filling with a touch of sweetness and citrus flavor. They make a delightful treat for any occasion!

Ovos Moles de Aveiro (Aveiro Soft Eggs)

Ingredients:

- 12 large egg yolks
- 1 cup (200g) granulated sugar
- 1/2 cup (120ml) water
- Pinch of salt
- Optional: cinnamon stick or citrus zest for flavoring

Instructions:

1. **Prepare the Syrup:**
    - In a saucepan, combine the sugar and water over medium heat. Stir until the sugar dissolves completely.
    - If using, add a cinnamon stick or citrus zest to infuse flavor into the syrup. Bring to a gentle boil, then reduce the heat and simmer for 5 minutes. Remove from heat and set aside to cool slightly.
2. **Make the Ovos Moles:**
    - In a heatproof bowl, whisk the egg yolks until smooth.
    - Slowly pour the warm sugar syrup into the egg yolks, whisking constantly to incorporate. Be careful not to cook the egg yolks; the syrup should be warm but not hot.
    - Place the bowl over a pot of simmering water (double boiler method) and continue whisking constantly until the mixture thickens and coats the back of a spoon. This will take about 10-15 minutes. The mixture should be smooth and velvety.
3. **Cool and Serve:**
    - Remove the bowl from the heat and let the Ovos Moles cool to room temperature.
    - Transfer the Ovos Moles to individual serving dishes or jars. You can strain the mixture through a fine sieve if you prefer a smoother texture.
    - Chill in the refrigerator for at least 1 hour before serving. The Ovos Moles will thicken further as they cool.
4. **Serve:**
    - Serve Ovos Moles de Aveiro chilled. They can be enjoyed on their own as a dessert or used as a filling for pastries and cakes.

Tips:

- The key to making smooth and creamy Ovos Moles is to whisk the egg yolks continuously and to gradually incorporate the warm sugar syrup.
- Adjust the sweetness to your taste by adding more or less sugar.

- Ovos Moles de Aveiro are traditionally served in small decorative molds or wrapped in edible rice paper for a beautiful presentation.

Enjoy this classic Portuguese dessert, Ovos Moles de Aveiro, and savor its rich, velvety texture and delicate sweetness that embodies the culinary heritage of Aveiro!

Bolinhos de Amêndoa (Portuguese Almond Cookies)

Ingredients:

- 250g (about 2 cups) almond flour or finely ground almonds
- 200g (about 1 cup) granulated sugar
- 2 large egg whites
- 1/2 tsp almond extract (optional)
- Pinch of salt
- Whole almonds, for decoration (optional)

Instructions:

1. **Preheat the Oven:**
    - Preheat your oven to 350°F (175°C). Line a baking sheet with parchment paper.
2. **Prepare the Dough:**
    - In a large mixing bowl, combine the almond flour (or ground almonds) and granulated sugar. Mix well.
    - Add the egg whites, almond extract (if using), and a pinch of salt to the almond mixture. Mix until a thick, sticky dough forms. You can use a spoon or your hands to mix the dough thoroughly.
3. **Shape the Cookies:**
    - Take small portions of the dough (about 1 tablespoon each) and roll them into balls.
    - Place the balls on the prepared baking sheet, spacing them a few inches apart. Press a whole almond into the center of each cookie, if desired, for decoration.
4. **Bake the Cookies:**
    - Bake in the preheated oven for 12-15 minutes, or until the cookies are lightly golden brown around the edges.
5. **Cooling:**
    - Remove the cookies from the oven and let them cool on the baking sheet for a few minutes.
    - Transfer the cookies to a wire rack to cool completely. They will firm up as they cool.
6. **Serve:**
    - Once completely cooled, store the Bolinhos de Amêndoa in an airtight container at room temperature.

Tips:

- If you use almond flour, the cookies will have a finer texture. If you use ground almonds, they will have a slightly more rustic texture.
- You can adjust the sweetness by adding more or less sugar, according to your preference.

- These cookies are naturally gluten-free, making them suitable for those with gluten intolerance or celiac disease.

Enjoy these Bolinhos de Amêndoa with a cup of tea or coffee, or as a sweet treat any time of day. They capture the delicious essence of Portuguese almond cookies, perfect for sharing with family and friends!

Bolo Rei (Portuguese King Cake)

Ingredients:

For the Dough:

- 500g (4 cups) bread flour
- 100g (1/2 cup) granulated sugar
- 10g (2 tsp) active dry yeast
- 100ml (1/2 cup) lukewarm milk
- 100g (7 tbsp) unsalted butter, softened
- 3 large eggs
- Zest of 1 lemon
- Zest of 1 orange
- 1/2 tsp salt

For the Filling:

- 150g (1 cup) raisins
- 100g (1/2 cup) candied fruit (such as orange peel, lemon peel, cherries)
- 50ml (1/4 cup) Port wine or rum

For Decoration:

- Candied fruits (cherries, figs, etc.)
- Whole almonds
- Powdered sugar, for dusting

For Glaze:

- 100g (3/4 cup) powdered sugar
- 2-3 tbsp water

Instructions:

1. **Prepare the Filling:**
    - In a small bowl, combine the raisins, candied fruit, and Port wine (or rum). Let them soak for at least 1 hour, preferably overnight, until the fruits are plump and infused with flavor.
2. **Make the Dough:**
    - In a large mixing bowl, combine the lukewarm milk and yeast. Let it sit for 5-10 minutes until frothy.
    - Add the flour, sugar, softened butter, eggs, lemon zest, orange zest, and salt to the yeast mixture.

- Mix everything together until a dough forms. You can knead the dough by hand on a lightly floured surface or use a stand mixer with a dough hook attachment.
- Knead the dough for about 10 minutes, until it becomes smooth and elastic.
- Drain the soaked fruits and add them to the dough. Knead the dough again to evenly distribute the fruits.
- Place the dough in a large bowl, cover with plastic wrap or a kitchen towel, and let it rise in a warm place for about 1-2 hours, or until doubled in size.

3. **Shape the Cake:**
    - Once the dough has risen, punch it down gently to deflate.
    - Divide the dough into two equal portions. Take one portion and divide it into three smaller portions (for the braids).
    - Roll each portion into a long rope, about 16-18 inches (40-45 cm) long.
    - Braid the three ropes together, pinching the ends to seal and form a braided ring. Place the ring on a baking sheet lined with parchment paper.
    - Repeat with the second portion of dough to make another braided ring.

4. **Decorate:**
    - Preheat your oven to 350°F (175°C).
    - Decorate the tops of the Bolo Rei with candied fruits and whole almonds, pressing them lightly into the dough.

5. **Bake:**
    - Cover the Bolo Rei loosely with plastic wrap or a clean kitchen towel and let them rise again for about 30 minutes.
    - Bake in the preheated oven for 25-30 minutes, or until golden brown on top and cooked through. If the tops start to brown too quickly, you can cover them loosely with aluminum foil halfway through baking.

6. **Glaze:**
    - While the Bolo Rei is baking, prepare the glaze. In a small bowl, whisk together the powdered sugar and water until smooth.
    - Once the Bolo Rei is done baking, remove it from the oven and immediately brush the glaze over the warm cakes.

7. **Serve:**
    - Let the Bolo Rei cool completely on a wire rack before serving.
    - Dust with powdered sugar before serving for an extra festive touch.

Tips:

- Bolo Rei is best enjoyed fresh, but it can be stored in an airtight container at room temperature for a few days.
- You can customize the filling by adding chopped nuts or other dried fruits like apricots or figs.
- Traditionally, a small token or charm (like a dried bean or figurine) is hidden inside the Bolo Rei before baking. The person who finds it in their slice is considered lucky and traditionally has to buy the Bolo Rei the following year.

Bolo Rei is a beautiful and delicious centerpiece for any Christmas celebration, embodying the rich culinary tradition of Portugal. Enjoy this festive cake with family and friends during the holiday season!

Fatias Douradas (Portuguese Golden Slices)

Ingredients:

- 4 slices of day-old bread (preferably Portuguese or French bread)
- 4 large eggs
- 1 cup (240ml) milk
- 1/4 cup (50g) granulated sugar
- Zest of 1 lemon
- 1 cinnamon stick (or 1 tsp ground cinnamon)
- Pinch of salt
- Vegetable oil, for frying
- Cinnamon sugar or powdered sugar, for dusting (optional)

Instructions:

1. **Prepare the Bread:**
   - If using fresh bread, leave it out overnight to stale slightly. Alternatively, lightly toast the bread slices until they are dry but not browned.
2. **Make the Egg Mixture:**
   - In a shallow dish or bowl, whisk together the eggs, milk, granulated sugar, lemon zest, cinnamon (either ground or the cinnamon stick broken into pieces), and a pinch of salt.
3. **Soak the Bread:**
   - Dip each bread slice into the egg mixture, ensuring both sides are well coated. Let the bread soak for a few seconds to absorb the liquid.
4. **Fry the Fatias Douradas:**
   - Heat a large skillet or frying pan over medium heat. Add enough vegetable oil to coat the bottom of the pan.
   - Place the soaked bread slices in the skillet and fry them until golden brown on both sides, about 2-3 minutes per side. Adjust the heat as needed to prevent burning.
5. **Drain and Serve:**
   - Remove the Fatias Douradas from the skillet and drain them on paper towels to remove excess oil.
   - Optionally, sprinkle the Fatias Douradas with cinnamon sugar or powdered sugar for extra sweetness.
6. **Serve:**
   - Serve the Fatias Douradas warm. They can be enjoyed on their own or accompanied by a sprinkle of cinnamon sugar, powdered sugar, or even a drizzle of honey.

Tips:

- For a richer flavor, you can add a splash of vanilla extract or a pinch of nutmeg to the egg mixture.
- If you prefer a lighter version, you can use low-fat milk instead of whole milk.
- Fatias Douradas are versatile and can be served as a dessert or a sweet breakfast treat.

Enjoy these delicious Fatias Douradas as a taste of Portuguese tradition, perfect for indulging in a comforting and satisfying sweet treat!

Bolos de Arroz (Portuguese Rice Muffins)

Ingredients:

- 1/2 cup (100g) unsalted butter, softened
- 1/2 cup (100g) granulated sugar
- 2 large eggs
- 1/2 cup (70g) rice flour
- 1/2 cup (70g) all-purpose flour
- 1 tsp baking powder
- 1/4 cup (60ml) milk
- Zest of 1 lemon (optional)
- Pinch of salt
- Whole blanched almonds (optional, for decoration)
- Muffin/cupcake liners

Instructions:

1. **Preheat the Oven:**
    - Preheat your oven to 350°F (175°C). Line a muffin tin with muffin liners.
2. **Cream Butter and Sugar:**
    - In a mixing bowl, cream together the softened butter and granulated sugar until light and fluffy.
3. **Add Eggs:**
    - Add the eggs one at a time, mixing well after each addition.
4. **Combine Dry Ingredients:**
    - In a separate bowl, whisk together the rice flour, all-purpose flour, baking powder, and a pinch of salt.
5. **Mix Batter:**
    - Gradually add the dry ingredients to the butter-sugar-egg mixture, alternating with the milk. Mix until just combined. Be careful not to overmix.
6. **Add Lemon Zest (Optional):**
    - Fold in the lemon zest, if using, to add a hint of citrus flavor.
7. **Fill Muffin Tin:**
    - Spoon the batter into the prepared muffin tin, filling each liner about 2/3 full.
8. **Add Almonds (Optional):**
    - If desired, place a whole blanched almond on top of each muffin for decoration.
9. **Bake:**
    - Bake in the preheated oven for 20-25 minutes, or until the tops are lightly golden brown and a toothpick inserted into the center comes out clean.
10. **Cool and Serve:**
    - Remove the muffins from the oven and let them cool in the tin for a few minutes.
    - Transfer the muffins to a wire rack to cool completely.
11. **Serve:**

    - Enjoy Bolos de Arroz warm or at room temperature with a cup of coffee or tea.

Tips:

- Rice flour gives Bolos de Arroz their distinctive texture. If you can't find rice flour, you can try making your own by grinding raw rice in a blender or food processor until fine.
- These muffins are best enjoyed fresh on the day they are made but can be stored in an airtight container at room temperature for a few days.
- Bolos de Arroz are a wonderful treat for breakfast, snack time, or any special occasion. Their unique texture and flavor make them a favorite among Portuguese pastries.

Try making these Bolos de Arroz at home to experience a taste of Portuguese baking tradition!

Pudim Abade de Priscos (Abbot of Priscos Pudding)

Ingredients:

- 12 egg yolks
- 1 whole egg
- 300g (1 1/2 cups) granulated sugar
- 200ml (3/4 cup + 1 tbsp) water
- 1 cinnamon stick
- Zest of 1 lemon
- 1 tbsp butter, softened, for greasing the mold

Instructions:

1. **Prepare the Caramel:**
   - In a small saucepan, combine 200g (1 cup) of the sugar and water. Place over medium heat.
   - Stir until the sugar dissolves, then add the cinnamon stick and lemon zest.
   - Bring to a boil and simmer gently for about 15 minutes, until the syrup thickens slightly and turns a light caramel color. Remove from heat and let it cool slightly.
2. **Prepare the Pudding Mold:**
   - While the caramel is cooking, generously grease a pudding mold or a bundt pan with the softened butter. Make sure to coat the sides and bottom evenly.
   - Pour the caramel into the greased mold, swirling to coat the bottom and sides evenly. Set aside.
3. **Make the Pudding Mixture:**
   - In a large mixing bowl, whisk together the egg yolks, whole egg, and remaining 100g (1/2 cup) of sugar until well combined and creamy.
   - Gradually pour the cooled caramel syrup (remove the cinnamon stick and lemon zest) into the egg mixture, whisking constantly until well incorporated.
4. **Bake the Pudding:**
   - Preheat your oven to 350°F (175°C).
   - Pour the pudding mixture into the prepared caramel-coated mold.
   - Place the mold in a larger baking dish and fill the dish with hot water halfway up the sides of the mold (creating a water bath or bain-marie).
   - Bake in the preheated oven for about 1 hour to 1 hour and 15 minutes, or until the pudding is set and a toothpick inserted into the center comes out clean.
5. **Cooling and Serving:**
   - Remove the mold from the water bath and let the pudding cool to room temperature.
   - Once cooled, refrigerate the pudding for at least 4 hours or overnight to chill and set completely.
6. **Unmolding:**

- To unmold, run a knife around the edges of the pudding to loosen it from the mold.
- Place a serving plate upside down over the mold and carefully invert it. The caramel sauce will flow over the pudding, creating a delicious glaze.

7. **Serve:**
   - Slice and serve Pudim Abade de Priscos chilled, garnished with fresh berries or whipped cream if desired.

Tips:

- Pudim Abade de Priscos is best served chilled, allowing the flavors to develop fully.
- The caramel syrup should be cooked until it reaches a light caramel color to ensure the right flavor and consistency.
- This pudding is quite rich due to the use of egg yolks and sugar, making it a decadent and indulgent dessert.

Enjoy this classic Portuguese dessert, Pudim Abade de Priscos, which showcases the richness of Portuguese culinary tradition and is sure to impress with its luxurious taste and texture!

Barrigas de Freira (Nun's Bellies)

Ingredients:

For the Dough:

- 250g (about 2 cups) all-purpose flour
- 100g (1/2 cup) unsalted butter, softened
- 2 large eggs
- Pinch of salt
- Cold water, as needed

For the Filling:

- 6 large egg yolks
- 300g (1 1/2 cups) granulated sugar
- 250ml (1 cup) water
- 1 cinnamon stick
- Zest of 1 lemon

For Dusting:

- Powdered sugar, for dusting

Instructions:

1. **Prepare the Dough:**
   - In a large mixing bowl, combine the flour and salt. Add the softened butter and eggs, and mix until the dough starts to come together.
   - Gradually add cold water, a tablespoon at a time, if needed, to bring the dough together into a smooth and slightly sticky ball. Cover the dough with plastic wrap and refrigerate for 30 minutes.
2. **Make the Filling:**
   - In a saucepan, combine the sugar, water, cinnamon stick, and lemon zest. Bring to a boil over medium heat, stirring occasionally, until the sugar is dissolved.
   - Reduce the heat to low and simmer the syrup for about 10 minutes, until slightly thickened. Remove from heat and let it cool slightly.
   - In a separate bowl, whisk the egg yolks until smooth. Slowly pour the cooled syrup into the egg yolks, whisking constantly to temper the eggs.
   - Return the mixture to the saucepan and cook over low heat, stirring constantly, until it thickens and coats the back of a spoon (about 8-10 minutes). Remove from heat and let it cool completely.
3. **Assemble the Barrigas de Freira:**
   - Preheat your oven to 350°F (175°C). Grease a baking sheet or line it with parchment paper.

- On a lightly floured surface, roll out the chilled dough to a thickness of about 1/8 inch (3mm).
- Using a round cookie cutter or a glass, cut out circles of dough about 3 inches (7-8 cm) in diameter.
- Place a spoonful of the cooled filling in the center of each circle of dough. Fold the dough over to form a half-moon shape, pressing the edges firmly to seal. You can crimp the edges with a fork for decoration, if desired.
- Place the filled Barrigas de Freira on the prepared baking sheet, leaving some space between each one.

4. **Bake:**
    - Bake in the preheated oven for 15-20 minutes, or until the Barrigas de Freira are golden brown.
5. **Cool and Serve:**
    - Remove from the oven and let them cool on a wire rack.
    - Dust with powdered sugar before serving, if desired.

Tips:

- The filling should be thick enough to hold its shape when spooned onto the dough circles.
- Be careful not to overfill the Barrigas de Freira to avoid leakage during baking.
- These pastries are best enjoyed fresh on the day they are made, but they can be stored in an airtight container at room temperature for a day or two.

Barrigas de Freira are a delicious representation of Portuguese pastry tradition, combining a tender dough with a sweet, cinnamon-infused filling. Enjoy these delightful treats with a cup of coffee or tea for a truly authentic experience!

Broa de Avintes (Avintes Cornbread)

Ingredients:

- 250g (about 2 cups) fine cornmeal (corn flour)
- 250g (about 2 cups) all-purpose flour
- 1 tsp salt
- 1 tbsp granulated sugar
- 1 tbsp active dry yeast
- 300ml (1 1/4 cups) warm water
- 100ml (1/2 cup) olive oil
- Corn flour or extra cornmeal, for dusting

Instructions:

1. **Activate the Yeast:**
   - In a small bowl, combine the active dry yeast, warm water, and granulated sugar. Stir gently and let it sit for about 5-10 minutes until the mixture becomes frothy.
2. **Prepare the Dough:**
   - In a large mixing bowl, combine the fine cornmeal, all-purpose flour, and salt.
   - Make a well in the center of the flour mixture and pour in the activated yeast mixture and olive oil.
   - Mix everything together with a wooden spoon or your hands until a dough forms. If the dough is too sticky, add a little more flour; if it's too dry, add a little more water.
3. **Knead the Dough:**
   - Transfer the dough to a lightly floured surface and knead it for about 10-12 minutes, until it becomes smooth and elastic.
4. **First Rise:**
   - Place the dough in a clean, lightly oiled bowl. Cover the bowl with a kitchen towel or plastic wrap and let it rise in a warm place for about 1 hour, or until doubled in size.
5. **Shape the Broa:**
   - Preheat your oven to 375°F (190°C). Line a baking sheet with parchment paper and dust it lightly with corn flour or extra cornmeal.
   - Punch down the risen dough and shape it into a round or oval loaf, about 8-10 inches (20-25 cm) in diameter.
   - Place the shaped dough onto the prepared baking sheet. Dust the top with a little more corn flour or cornmeal.
6. **Second Rise:**
   - Cover the shaped Broa loosely with a clean kitchen towel and let it rise again for about 30 minutes.
7. **Bake:**

        - Bake the Broa in the preheated oven for 35-40 minutes, or until it is golden brown and sounds hollow when tapped on the bottom.
8. **Cooling and Serving:**
    - Remove the Broa from the oven and let it cool on a wire rack before slicing and serving.

Tips:

- Broa de Avintes is traditionally served with butter, cheese, or as an accompaniment to soups and stews.
- The texture of Broa can vary from dense to slightly airy, depending on personal preference and regional variations.
- Store any leftovers in an airtight container at room temperature for a few days, or freeze slices for longer storage.

Enjoy the rustic and hearty flavors of Broa de Avintes, a beloved traditional Portuguese cornbread that pairs perfectly with a variety of dishes or simply on its own!

Bolinhos de Coco (Portuguese Coconut Cookies)

Ingredients:

- 200g (about 2 cups) sweetened shredded coconut
- 100g (about 1 cup) granulated sugar
- 2 large eggs
- 1/4 cup (60ml) milk
- 50g (1/4 cup) unsalted butter, melted
- 1/2 tsp vanilla extract
- Pinch of salt
- Zest of 1 lemon (optional)
- 100g (about 3/4 cup) all-purpose flour
- 1 tsp baking powder

Instructions:

1. **Preheat the Oven:**
   - Preheat your oven to 350°F (175°C). Line a baking sheet with parchment paper.
2. **Mix Coconut and Sugar:**
   - In a large mixing bowl, combine the sweetened shredded coconut and granulated sugar. Mix well to combine.
3. **Add Wet Ingredients:**
   - Add the eggs, milk, melted butter, vanilla extract, and lemon zest (if using) to the coconut-sugar mixture. Mix until well combined.
4. **Combine Dry Ingredients:**
   - In a separate bowl, sift together the all-purpose flour, baking powder, and a pinch of salt.
5. **Mix Everything Together:**
   - Gradually add the dry ingredients to the wet ingredients, mixing until a sticky dough forms.
6. **Shape the Cookies:**
   - Using a spoon or cookie scoop, drop tablespoon-sized portions of dough onto the prepared baking sheet, spacing them a few inches apart.
7. **Bake:**
   - Bake in the preheated oven for 12-15 minutes, or until the edges of the cookies are lightly golden brown.
8. **Cool and Serve:**
   - Remove the cookies from the oven and let them cool on the baking sheet for a few minutes.
   - Transfer the cookies to a wire rack to cool completely.

Tips:

- For extra coconut flavor, you can toast the shredded coconut before adding it to the cookie dough. Simply spread the coconut on a baking sheet and bake at 350°F (175°C) for 5-7 minutes, stirring occasionally, until lightly golden brown.
- These Bolinhos de Coco are best enjoyed fresh, but they can be stored in an airtight container at room temperature for several days.
- You can customize these cookies by adding chocolate chips, chopped nuts, or dried fruit to the dough for added texture and flavor.

Enjoy these Bolinhos de Coco as a delightful treat with a cup of tea or coffee, or share them with friends and family for a taste of Portuguese sweetness!

Coscorões (Portuguese Fried Pastry)

Ingredients:

- 500g (4 cups) all-purpose flour
- 4 large eggs
- 50g (1/4 cup) granulated sugar
- Zest of 1 lemon
- Zest of 1 orange
- 1/2 tsp baking powder
- Pinch of salt
- 50g (3 1/2 tbsp) unsalted butter, melted
- Vegetable oil, for frying
- Cinnamon sugar, for dusting (optional)

Instructions:

1. **Prepare the Dough:**
   - In a large mixing bowl, combine the flour, granulated sugar, lemon zest, orange zest, baking powder, and a pinch of salt.
   - Make a well in the center of the dry ingredients and add the eggs and melted butter.
   - Mix everything together until a dough forms. If the dough is too dry, add a little bit of water, a tablespoon at a time, until the dough comes together smoothly. It should be soft and slightly sticky.
2. **Knead the Dough:**
   - Turn the dough out onto a lightly floured surface and knead it for about 5-7 minutes, until it becomes smooth and elastic.
3. **Rest the Dough:**
   - Cover the dough with plastic wrap or a clean kitchen towel and let it rest at room temperature for about 30 minutes to relax the gluten.
4. **Roll and Cut the Coscorões:**
   - After resting, roll out the dough on a lightly floured surface to a thickness of about 1/4 inch (6-7 mm).
   - Use a sharp knife or a pastry cutter to cut the dough into rectangles or diamond shapes, about 2-3 inches (5-7 cm) long and 1 inch (2-3 cm) wide.
5. **Fry the Coscorões:**
   - In a deep, heavy-bottomed pot or a deep fryer, heat vegetable oil to 350°F (175°C).
   - Carefully add a few pieces of dough to the hot oil, being careful not to overcrowd the pot. Fry them in batches for about 2-3 minutes on each side, or until they are golden brown and puffed up.
   - Use a slotted spoon or tongs to transfer the fried Coscorões to a plate lined with paper towels to drain excess oil.

6. **Serve:**
    - While still warm, dust the Coscorões with cinnamon sugar, if desired.
7. **Enjoy:**
    - Serve Coscorões warm or at room temperature as a festive treat. They are best enjoyed fresh on the day they are made.

Tips:

- Make sure the oil is at the correct temperature before frying to ensure that the Coscorões cook evenly and become crispy on the outside.
- You can adjust the thickness and size of the Coscorões according to your preference. Thicker pieces will be softer inside, while thinner pieces will be crispier.
- Store any leftovers in an airtight container at room temperature. They can be reheated briefly in the oven to restore their crispness.

Enjoy making and sharing these traditional Portuguese Coscorões with family and friends during special occasions or as a delightful treat any time of the year!

Pão-de-Ló de Margaride (Margaride Sponge Cake)

Ingredients:

- 6 large eggs, at room temperature
- 200g (1 cup) granulated sugar
- 100g (3/4 cup) cake flour
- 1/2 tsp baking powder
- Zest of 1 lemon (optional)
- Butter and flour, for greasing the pan
- Powdered sugar, for dusting (optional)

Instructions:

1. **Prepare the Pan:**
   - Preheat your oven to 350°F (175°C). Grease a round cake pan (about 8-9 inches/20-23 cm in diameter) with butter and dust it lightly with flour, tapping out any excess.
2. **Whip the Eggs and Sugar:**
   - In a large mixing bowl, using an electric mixer or stand mixer fitted with the whisk attachment, beat the eggs and granulated sugar together on medium-high speed for about 10-12 minutes, or until the mixture is thick, pale yellow, and tripled in volume. The mixture should form ribbons when you lift the beaters.
3. **Sift Dry Ingredients:**
   - In a separate bowl, sift together the cake flour and baking powder. If using, add the lemon zest to the flour mixture and gently mix.
4. **Fold Dry Ingredients:**
   - Gradually sift and fold the dry ingredients into the egg-sugar mixture in three additions, using a spatula. Be gentle to avoid deflating the batter, but make sure the flour is fully incorporated.
5. **Bake:**
   - Pour the batter into the prepared cake pan and gently tap the pan on the counter to remove any air bubbles.
   - Bake in the preheated oven for 25-30 minutes, or until the top is golden brown and a toothpick inserted into the center comes out clean.
6. **Cooling:**
   - Remove the cake from the oven and let it cool in the pan for about 10 minutes.
   - Carefully run a knife around the edges of the cake to loosen it, then transfer it to a wire rack to cool completely.
7. **Serve:**
   - Once cooled, dust the top of the Pão-de-Ló de Margaride with powdered sugar, if desired.
8. **Enjoy:**

- Slice and serve the sponge cake on its own or with fresh fruit, whipped cream, or a scoop of ice cream.

Tips:

- For a richer flavor, you can add a splash of vanilla extract or a pinch of salt to the batter.
- Make sure the eggs are at room temperature before beating to achieve maximum volume.
- Store any leftovers in an airtight container at room temperature for up to 2 days, or refrigerate for longer freshness.

Pão-de-Ló de Margaride is a classic Portuguese dessert that showcases the simplicity and elegance of traditional sponge cakes. Enjoy its delicate texture and subtle sweetness with a cup of coffee or tea for a delightful treat!

Folares (Portuguese Easter Bread)

Ingredients:

- 500g (about 4 cups) all-purpose flour
- 100g (about 1/2 cup) granulated sugar
- 2 tsp active dry yeast
- 1/2 tsp salt
- Zest of 1 lemon
- Zest of 1 orange
- 3 large eggs, plus 1 egg for egg wash
- 100ml (about 1/2 cup) warm milk
- 100g (7 tbsp) unsalted butter, softened
- 100g (about 1/2 cup) raisins (optional)
- Hard-boiled eggs, peeled (optional, for decoration)
- Powdered sugar, for dusting (optional)

Instructions:

1. **Activate the Yeast:**
    - In a small bowl, dissolve 1 tsp of sugar in the warm milk. Sprinkle the yeast over the milk mixture and let it sit for about 5-10 minutes, until foamy.
2. **Mix Dough:**
    - In a large mixing bowl, combine the flour, remaining sugar, salt, lemon zest, and orange zest. Make a well in the center and add the yeast mixture, eggs, and softened butter.
    - Mix everything together until a dough forms. If using raisins, knead them into the dough until evenly distributed.
3. **Knead and Rise:**
    - Turn the dough out onto a lightly floured surface and knead for about 10 minutes, until smooth and elastic.
    - Place the dough in a clean, lightly oiled bowl. Cover with a kitchen towel or plastic wrap and let it rise in a warm place for about 1 to 1.5 hours, or until doubled in size.
4. **Shape the Folares:**
    - After rising, punch down the dough and divide it into portions, depending on how many Folares you want to make. Traditional shapes include round loaves or braided breads.
    - If using hard-boiled eggs, gently press them into the dough for decoration.
5. **Second Rise:**
    - Place the shaped Folares on a baking sheet lined with parchment paper. Cover loosely with a kitchen towel and let them rise again for about 30-45 minutes.
6. **Preheat and Bake:**

- Preheat your oven to 350°F (175°C). Beat the remaining egg and brush it over the risen Folares for a golden finish.
- Bake the Folares in the preheated oven for 25-30 minutes, or until they are golden brown and sound hollow when tapped on the bottom.

7. **Cool and Serve:**
    - Remove the Folares from the oven and let them cool on a wire rack.
    - Optional: Dust with powdered sugar for decoration before serving.

Tips:

- Folares can be customized with different fillings such as ham, chorizo, or even sweet fillings like cinnamon sugar.
- Ensure the yeast is activated properly to ensure a good rise.
- Enjoy Folares fresh on the day they are made, or warm them briefly in the oven before serving the next day.

Folares are a delightful symbol of Easter celebrations in Portugal, combining tradition, symbolism, and delicious flavors into a festive bread that can be enjoyed with family and friends.

Lampreia de Ovos (Portuguese Egg Lamprey)

Ingredients:

- 12 large egg yolks
- 300g (1 1/2 cups) granulated sugar
- Water, as needed

Instructions:

1. **Prepare the Syrup:**
   - In a saucepan, combine the sugar with just enough water to cover it (about 1/2 cup). Stir over medium heat until the sugar dissolves completely.
   - Once the sugar has dissolved, stop stirring and bring the syrup to a boil. Reduce the heat and let it simmer until it reaches the thread stage (approximately 110°C/230°F on a candy thermometer). Remove from heat and set aside to cool slightly.
2. **Whisk the Egg Yolks:**
   - In a large mixing bowl, whisk the egg yolks until smooth and creamy.
3. **Add the Syrup:**
   - Gradually add the cooled syrup to the egg yolks, whisking constantly. Continue adding the syrup until it is fully incorporated and the mixture thickens.
4. **Cook the Mixture:**
   - Pour the egg yolk mixture into a clean saucepan. Cook over low heat, stirring constantly with a wooden spoon or silicone spatula, until the mixture thickens enough to coat the back of the spoon. Be careful not to let it boil or the yolks will curdle.
5. **Shape the Lampreia:**
   - Remove the saucepan from the heat and let the mixture cool slightly.
   - Prepare a lamprey-shaped mold or use a shallow dish lined with parchment paper or plastic wrap. Pour the egg yolk mixture into the mold, spreading it evenly with a spatula.
6. **Chill and Serve:**
   - Refrigerate the Lampreia de Ovos for at least 4-6 hours, or overnight, until it sets completely.
   - Once set, carefully unmold the Lampreia de Ovos onto a serving platter.
7. **Decorate (Optional):**
   - You can decorate the Lampreia de Ovos with additional egg yolks, using a pastry bag fitted with a small round tip to pipe patterns on top.
8. **Serve:**
   - Slice and serve the Lampreia de Ovos chilled. It's a rich and indulgent dessert, often served in small portions due to its sweetness.

Tips:

- The traditional lamprey shape can be achieved by using a special lamprey mold, which is shaped like a fish. If you don't have a mold, you can use a shallow dish and shape it by hand.
- Be patient when adding the sugar syrup to the egg yolks, as adding it too quickly can cause the yolks to curdle.
- Lampreia de Ovos is a decadent dessert, so small slices are typically served.

Enjoy this classic Portuguese dessert, Lampreia de Ovos, which showcases the richness of egg yolks and the culinary traditions of Portugal!

Azevias de Grão (Chickpea Turnovers)

Ingredients:

For the Dough:

- 300g (about 2 1/2 cups) all-purpose flour
- 100g (7 tbsp) unsalted butter, softened
- 1/4 tsp salt
- 1/4 cup cold water, or as needed

For the Filling:

- 250g (about 1 1/4 cups) cooked chickpeas (canned or cooked from dry)
- 150g (3/4 cup) granulated sugar
- Zest of 1 lemon
- 1/2 tsp ground cinnamon
- 1/4 tsp ground nutmeg
- Pinch of salt
- 50g (3 1/2 tbsp) unsalted butter, melted
- Vegetable oil, for frying
- Powdered sugar, for dusting

Instructions:

1. **Prepare the Dough:**
   - In a large mixing bowl, combine the flour and salt. Add the softened butter and rub it into the flour mixture until it resembles breadcrumbs.
   - Gradually add cold water, a little at a time, mixing until the dough comes together. You may not need to use all the water. Knead the dough until smooth and elastic. Wrap it in plastic wrap and refrigerate for at least 30 minutes.
2. **Make the Filling:**
   - In a food processor, blend the cooked chickpeas until smooth.
   - In a saucepan, combine the chickpea puree, granulated sugar, lemon zest, cinnamon, nutmeg, and a pinch of salt. Cook over medium heat, stirring constantly, until the mixture thickens and pulls away from the sides of the pan (about 10-15 minutes).
   - Remove from heat and stir in the melted butter until well combined. Let the filling cool completely.
3. **Shape and Fill the Turnovers:**
   - On a lightly floured surface, roll out the chilled dough to a thickness of about 1/8 inch (3mm). Using a round cookie cutter or a glass, cut out circles of dough about 3-4 inches (7-10 cm) in diameter.

- Place a spoonful of the cooled chickpea filling onto one half of each dough circle. Fold the other half of the dough over the filling to form a turnover. Press the edges firmly to seal, and crimp the edges with a fork for decoration.
4. **Fry the Azevias:**
    - In a deep, heavy-bottomed pot, heat vegetable oil to 350°F (175°C).
    - Carefully add a few turnovers at a time to the hot oil, frying until golden brown on both sides (about 2-3 minutes per side).
    - Remove the fried turnovers with a slotted spoon and drain on paper towels to remove excess oil.
5. **Serve:**
    - Let the Azevias de Grão cool slightly before dusting with powdered sugar.
    - Serve warm or at room temperature. They are best enjoyed fresh on the day they are made.

Tips:

- Ensure the chickpea filling is thick and cool before filling the turnovers to prevent them from becoming soggy.
- You can adjust the sweetness of the filling to your taste by adding more or less sugar.
- Store any leftover Azevias de Grão in an airtight container at room temperature for up to 2 days. Reheat briefly in the oven before serving to crisp them up.

Enjoy these delightful Azevias de Grão, filled with a sweet and spiced chickpea filling, as a special treat during festive seasons or any time you crave a taste of Portuguese tradition!

Pão de Ló de Ovar (Ovar Sponge Cake)

Ingredients:

- 12 large eggs, at room temperature
- 300g (1 1/2 cups) granulated sugar
- 150g (1 1/4 cups) cake flour
- Pinch of salt
- Zest of 1 lemon (optional)
- Butter and flour, for greasing the pan

Instructions:

1. **Prepare the Pan:**
   - Preheat your oven to 350°F (175°C). Grease a round cake pan (about 9 inches/23 cm in diameter) with butter and dust it lightly with flour, tapping out any excess.
2. **Whip the Eggs and Sugar:**
   - In a large mixing bowl, using an electric mixer or stand mixer fitted with the whisk attachment, beat the eggs and granulated sugar together on medium-high speed for about 15-20 minutes, or until the mixture is very thick, pale yellow, and tripled in volume. The mixture should form ribbons when you lift the beaters.
3. **Fold in the Dry Ingredients:**
   - Sift the cake flour and a pinch of salt over the whipped egg mixture. Add the lemon zest, if using.
   - Using a spatula, gently fold the flour into the egg mixture until just combined. Be careful not to deflate the batter too much.
4. **Bake:**
   - Pour the batter into the prepared cake pan. Gently tap the pan on the counter to remove any air bubbles.
   - Bake in the preheated oven for 30-35 minutes, or until the top is golden brown and a toothpick inserted into the center comes out clean.
5. **Cooling:**
   - Remove the cake from the oven and let it cool in the pan for about 10 minutes.
   - Carefully run a knife around the edges of the cake to loosen it, then transfer it to a wire rack to cool completely.
6. **Serve:**
   - Once cooled, slice and serve the Pão de Ló de Ovar on its own or with a dusting of powdered sugar.

Tips:

- Make sure the eggs are at room temperature before beating to achieve maximum volume.

- The cake flour helps to give the Pão de Ló its light and tender texture. If you don't have cake flour, you can make a substitute by replacing 2 tablespoons of flour with cornstarch for every cup of all-purpose flour.
- Pão de Ló de Ovar is traditionally served plain, without any frosting or filling, to highlight its delicate texture and flavor.

Enjoy this classic Portuguese dessert, Pão de Ló de Ovar, which is perfect for special occasions or as a delightful treat any time of the year!

Amêndoas de Cascais (Cascais Almonds)

Ingredients:

- 250g (about 2 cups) whole almonds, blanched
- 200g (1 cup) granulated sugar
- 100ml (1/2 cup) water
- 1/2 tsp vanilla extract
- Pinch of salt
- Vegetable oil, for greasing

Instructions:

1. **Prepare the Almonds:**
    - If your almonds still have skins, blanch them in boiling water for about 1-2 minutes, then drain and rinse with cold water. Pat dry with a clean kitchen towel to remove excess moisture.
2. **Make the Sugar Syrup:**
    - In a medium saucepan, combine the granulated sugar and water. Stir over medium heat until the sugar dissolves completely.
    - Bring the mixture to a boil, then reduce the heat to medium-low and let it simmer for about 5 minutes, until it reaches the soft-ball stage (about 115°C/240°F on a candy thermometer).
3. **Add Flavorings:**
    - Remove the sugar syrup from the heat and stir in the vanilla extract and a pinch of salt.
4. **Coat the Almonds:**
    - Add the blanched almonds to the sugar syrup, stirring quickly to coat them evenly.
    - Return the saucepan to medium heat. Cook the almonds, stirring constantly, until the syrup crystallizes and coats the almonds completely. This should take about 5-7 minutes.
5. **Cool and Separate:**
    - Transfer the coated almonds onto a greased baking sheet or parchment paper, spreading them out in a single layer to cool.
    - Allow the almonds to cool completely before breaking them apart if they stick together.
6. **Serve:**
    - Once cooled and separated, serve the Amêndoas de Cascais as a sweet treat. They can be stored in an airtight container at room temperature for several weeks.

Tips:

- Work quickly when coating the almonds in the sugar syrup, as it can harden fast once it reaches the crystallization point.
- You can customize the flavor of Amêndoas de Cascais by adding a touch of cinnamon or other spices to the sugar syrup.
- These almonds make a wonderful gift or party snack and are a delightful representation of Portuguese confectionery traditions.

Enjoy making and sharing these crunchy and sweet Amêndoas de Cascais with family and friends!

Leite Creme (Portuguese Cream)

Ingredients:

- 1 liter (4 1/4 cups) whole milk
- Zest of 1 lemon or 1 cinnamon stick (optional, for flavoring)
- 150g (3/4 cup) granulated sugar
- 6 large egg yolks
- 30g (1/4 cup) cornstarch
- 1 tsp vanilla extract
- Granulated sugar, for caramelizing

Instructions:

1. **Prepare the Milk Mixture:**
   - In a large saucepan, combine the milk and lemon zest or cinnamon stick (if using). Bring to a simmer over medium heat, stirring occasionally to prevent scorching. Once simmering, remove from heat and let it steep for about 10-15 minutes to infuse flavors. Remove lemon zest or cinnamon stick before proceeding.
2. **Mix the Egg Yolks:**
   - In a mixing bowl, whisk together the egg yolks and granulated sugar until pale and creamy.
3. **Thicken the Mixture:**
   - Add the cornstarch to the egg yolk mixture and whisk until smooth.
   - Gradually pour the warm milk into the egg yolk mixture, whisking constantly to combine.
4. **Cook the Custard:**
   - Pour the mixture back into the saucepan and return to medium heat. Cook, stirring constantly with a wooden spoon or silicone spatula, until the mixture thickens and coats the back of the spoon. This should take about 10-15 minutes. Do not let it boil.
   - Stir in the vanilla extract once the mixture has thickened.
5. **Chill the Custard:**
   - Remove the saucepan from the heat and pour the custard into individual ramekins or a shallow baking dish.
   - Let the Leite Creme cool to room temperature, then cover with plastic wrap directly on the surface of the custard to prevent a skin from forming. Refrigerate for at least 2-3 hours, or until chilled and set.
6. **Caramelize the Sugar:**
   - Just before serving, sprinkle a thin layer of granulated sugar evenly over the chilled Leite Creme.

- Use a kitchen torch to caramelize the sugar until it forms a golden-brown crust. Alternatively, you can place the ramekins under a broiler for a few minutes, watching carefully to avoid burning.

7. **Serve:**
    - Let the caramelized Leite Creme sit for a minute to allow the sugar to harden. Serve immediately, while the caramel crust is still crisp.

Tips:

- For a traditional touch, you can infuse the milk with lemon zest or a cinnamon stick. Both options add subtle flavors that complement the creamy custard.
- Be patient when cooking the custard on the stovetop; low to medium heat is key to prevent curdling and ensure a smooth texture.
- Adjust the sweetness by varying the amount of sugar used for caramelizing, depending on your preference.

Enjoy this creamy and caramelized Portuguese dessert, Leite Creme, as a delightful ending to any meal or festive occasion!

Folar de Olhão (Olhão Cake)

Ingredients:

For the Dough:

- 500g (about 4 cups) all-purpose flour
- 100g (about 1/2 cup) granulated sugar
- 100g (7 tbsp) unsalted butter, melted
- 2 large eggs, plus 1 egg yolk for brushing
- Zest of 1 lemon
- Zest of 1 orange
- 1/2 tsp ground cinnamon
- 1/4 tsp ground nutmeg
- 1/4 tsp salt
- 10g (2 tsp) active dry yeast
- 100ml (about 1/2 cup) warm milk

For the Filling:

- 200g (about 1 1/4 cups) granulated sugar
- 200g (1 3/4 cups) ground almonds
- 2 large eggs
- 2 tbsp unsalted butter, melted
- 1 tsp vanilla extract
- Zest of 1 lemon

For Decoration (Optional):

- Whole almonds or candied fruits for topping

Instructions:

1. **Prepare the Dough:**
    - In a small bowl, dissolve the yeast in the warm milk. Let it sit for about 5-10 minutes, until frothy.
    - In a large mixing bowl, combine the flour, sugar, lemon zest, orange zest, cinnamon, nutmeg, and salt. Make a well in the center and add the melted butter, eggs, and activated yeast mixture.
    - Mix everything together until a dough forms. Knead the dough on a lightly floured surface for about 10 minutes, until smooth and elastic.
    - Place the dough in a greased bowl, cover with a clean kitchen towel or plastic wrap, and let it rise in a warm place for about 1-1.5 hours, or until doubled in size.
2. **Make the Filling:**

- In a bowl, combine the granulated sugar, ground almonds, eggs, melted butter, vanilla extract, and lemon zest. Mix until well combined to form a thick paste.
3. **Assemble the Folar:**
    - Punch down the risen dough and divide it into two equal portions.
    - Roll out one portion of the dough on a lightly floured surface into a rectangle or oval shape, about 1/2 inch (1.5 cm) thick.
    - Spread half of the almond filling evenly over the rolled-out dough, leaving a border around the edges.
    - Roll out the second portion of dough into a similar shape and size, and place it over the almond filling. Press the edges together to seal.
4. **Bake:**
    - Preheat your oven to 350°F (175°C).
    - Transfer the assembled Folar de Olhão onto a baking sheet lined with parchment paper. Brush the top with the beaten egg yolk.
    - If desired, decorate the top with whole almonds or candied fruits.
    - Bake in the preheated oven for 30-35 minutes, or until golden brown and cooked through. If the top begins to brown too quickly, cover loosely with foil.
5. **Cool and Serve:**
    - Remove from the oven and let the Folar de Olhão cool on a wire rack.
    - Once cooled, slice and serve this delicious Portuguese cake. It can be enjoyed warm or at room temperature.

Tips:

- Adjust the sweetness of the filling to your preference by adding more or less sugar.
- You can also add a pinch of cinnamon or nutmeg to the filling for additional flavor.
- Folar de Olhão is best enjoyed fresh on the day it is made, but leftovers can be stored in an airtight container at room temperature for a couple of days.

Enjoy making and savoring Folar de Olhão, a delightful traditional cake that brings a taste of Portuguese culinary heritage to your table!

Coscoréis (Portuguese Fried Dough)

Ingredients:

- 500g (about 4 cups) all-purpose flour
- 100g (about 7 tbsp) unsalted butter, melted
- 4 large eggs
- 100ml (about 1/2 cup) white wine or port wine
- Zest of 1 lemon
- 1/2 tsp ground cinnamon
- 1/4 tsp salt
- Vegetable oil, for frying
- Granulated sugar, for dusting (optional)
- Honey, for drizzling (optional)

Instructions:

1. **Mix the Dough:**
    - In a large mixing bowl, combine the flour, melted butter, eggs, white wine, lemon zest, cinnamon, and salt. Mix well until a smooth dough forms. You can knead it by hand or use a stand mixer with a dough hook attachment.
2. **Rest the Dough:**
    - Cover the dough with plastic wrap or a clean kitchen towel and let it rest at room temperature for about 30 minutes to 1 hour.
3. **Roll and Cut the Dough:**
    - On a lightly floured surface, roll out the rested dough to a thickness of about 1/4 inch (0.5 cm).
    - Use a knife or a pastry wheel to cut the dough into rectangles or diamond shapes, about 3-4 inches (7-10 cm) long and 1 inch (2.5 cm) wide. You can also use cookie cutters for different shapes.
4. **Fry the Coscorões:**
    - In a large, deep skillet or pot, heat vegetable oil over medium-high heat until it reaches about 350°F (175°C).
    - Carefully add a few pieces of dough at a time to the hot oil, frying until golden brown and crispy on both sides, about 2-3 minutes per side. Use a slotted spoon or spider strainer to remove the Coscorões and transfer them to a plate lined with paper towels to drain excess oil.
5. **Serve:**
    - While still warm, dust the Coscorões with granulated sugar or drizzle them with honey for added sweetness, if desired.
6. **Storage:**
    - Coscorões are best enjoyed fresh on the day they are made. Store any leftovers in an airtight container at room temperature for up to 2 days.

Tips:

- Ensure the oil is at the right temperature before frying to achieve crispy Coscorões without absorbing too much oil.
- You can adjust the sweetness by varying the amount of sugar or honey used for dusting or drizzling.
- Coscorões are a delightful treat that brings a festive touch to any occasion, especially during the holiday season in Portugal.

Enjoy making and sharing these delicious Portuguese Coscorões with family and friends!

Biscoitos de Azeite (Portuguese Olive Oil Biscuits)

Ingredients:

- 250g (about 2 cups) all-purpose flour
- 100ml (about 1/2 cup) olive oil (use a good quality extra virgin olive oil for best flavor)
- 100g (about 1/2 cup) granulated sugar
- Zest of 1 lemon (optional)
- 1/2 tsp baking powder
- 1/4 tsp salt
- 1 large egg, lightly beaten (for brushing)
- Granulated sugar, for sprinkling (optional)

Instructions:

1. **Preheat the Oven:**
   - Preheat your oven to 350°F (175°C). Line a baking sheet with parchment paper.
2. **Mix the Dry Ingredients:**
   - In a large mixing bowl, whisk together the flour, granulated sugar, baking powder, salt, and lemon zest (if using).
3. **Add Olive Oil:**
   - Gradually add the olive oil to the dry ingredients, mixing with a spoon or your hands until the mixture resembles coarse crumbs and starts to come together.
4. **Form the Dough:**
   - Knead the dough gently in the bowl until it forms a smooth ball. If the dough is too crumbly, you can add a little more olive oil, a teaspoon at a time, until it holds together.
5. **Shape the Biscuits:**
   - Pinch off pieces of dough and roll them into small balls, about 1 inch (2.5 cm) in diameter. Place them on the prepared baking sheet, spacing them slightly apart.
6. **Brush with Egg Wash:**
   - Lightly beat the egg and brush the tops of the biscuits with it. This will give them a nice golden color when baked.
7. **Bake:**
   - Bake in the preheated oven for 15-20 minutes, or until the biscuits are lightly golden brown and firm to the touch.
8. **Optional Sugar Topping:**
   - If desired, sprinkle the tops of the biscuits with granulated sugar immediately after removing them from the oven. This adds a bit of sweetness and texture.
9. **Cool and Serve:**
   - Transfer the biscuits to a wire rack to cool completely. Once cooled, store them in an airtight container at room temperature.

Tips:

- You can customize the flavor of Biscoitos de Azeite by adding different citrus zests, such as orange or lime, or even a touch of cinnamon for a spiced variation.
- Be careful not to overwork the dough; just mix until it comes together to ensure a tender texture.
- These biscuits are perfect for enjoying with a cup of coffee or tea, or as a light snack any time of the day.

Enjoy making and savoring these delicious Portuguese Olive Oil Biscuits, a delightful treat that highlights the wonderful flavors of olive oil in baking!

Pão de Rala (Portuguese Bread of Rala)

Ingredients:

For the Dough:

- 250g (about 2 cups) finely ground almonds (almond flour)
- 250g (about 1 1/4 cups) granulated sugar
- 100g (about 1/2 cup) stale bread crumbs
- 6 large eggs
- Zest of 1 lemon
- 1/2 tsp ground cinnamon
- 1/4 tsp ground nutmeg
- Pinch of salt

For the Syrup:

- 200g (1 cup) granulated sugar
- 200ml (about 3/4 cup) water
- Zest of 1 lemon
- 1 cinnamon stick (optional)

Instructions:

1. **Prepare the Dough:**
    - In a large mixing bowl, combine the finely ground almonds, granulated sugar, stale bread crumbs, lemon zest, cinnamon, nutmeg, and a pinch of salt.
    - Separate the egg yolks from the whites. Beat the egg yolks until pale and creamy.
    - Gradually add the beaten egg yolks to the dry ingredients, mixing well to combine. The mixture should be thick and sticky.
    - In a separate bowl, beat the egg whites until stiff peaks form. Gently fold the beaten egg whites into the almond mixture until well incorporated.
2. **Bake:**
    - Preheat your oven to 350°F (175°C). Grease a round cake pan (about 9 inches/23 cm in diameter) with butter and dust it lightly with flour.
    - Pour the dough into the prepared cake pan, spreading it evenly with a spatula.
    - Bake in the preheated oven for about 30-35 minutes, or until the top is golden brown and a toothpick inserted into the center comes out clean.
3. **Make the Syrup:**
    - While the cake is baking, prepare the syrup. In a small saucepan, combine the granulated sugar, water, lemon zest, and cinnamon stick (if using).
    - Bring the mixture to a boil over medium heat, stirring occasionally until the sugar dissolves completely.

- Reduce the heat and let the syrup simmer for about 5-7 minutes, until slightly thickened. Remove from heat and discard the lemon zest and cinnamon stick.

4. **Soak the Cake:**
    - Once the cake is baked and while it's still warm, pierce the top of the cake with a skewer or toothpick in several places.
    - Slowly pour the warm syrup over the warm cake, allowing it to soak into the cake. Let the cake absorb the syrup and cool completely in the cake pan.

5. **Serve:**
    - Once cooled and soaked, remove the Pão de Rala from the cake pan and transfer it to a serving plate.
    - Cut into slices and serve at room temperature. It can be enjoyed on its own or with a cup of coffee or tea.

Tips:

- Make sure the stale bread crumbs are finely ground for a smooth texture in the cake.
- Adjust the sweetness of the syrup to your liking by adding more or less sugar.
- Pão de Rala is traditionally served at room temperature, allowing the flavors to develop fully.

Enjoy making and savoring this traditional Portuguese dessert, Pão de Rala, with its rich almond flavor and aromatic syrup!

Bolo de Noz (Portuguese Walnut Cake)

Ingredients:

- 200g (about 1 3/4 cups) walnuts, finely ground
- 200g (about 1 1/2 cups) all-purpose flour
- 200g (about 1 cup) granulated sugar
- 150g (about 2/3 cup) unsalted butter, softened
- 4 large eggs
- 1 tsp baking powder
- 1/2 tsp vanilla extract
- Zest of 1 lemon
- Pinch of salt

Instructions:

1. **Prepare the Walnuts:**
   - Preheat your oven to 350°F (175°C). Spread the walnuts evenly on a baking sheet and toast them in the oven for about 8-10 minutes, or until fragrant. Let them cool completely, then finely grind them in a food processor or blender.
2. **Prepare the Cake Batter:**
   - In a large mixing bowl, cream together the softened butter and granulated sugar until light and fluffy.
   - Add the eggs one at a time, beating well after each addition. Add the vanilla extract and lemon zest, and mix until combined.
   - In a separate bowl, whisk together the ground walnuts, all-purpose flour, baking powder, and a pinch of salt.
   - Gradually add the dry ingredients to the wet ingredients, mixing until just combined. Be careful not to overmix.
3. **Bake the Cake:**
   - Grease a round cake pan (about 9 inches/23 cm in diameter) with butter and dust it lightly with flour.
   - Pour the batter into the prepared cake pan, spreading it evenly with a spatula.
   - Bake in the preheated oven for 30-35 minutes, or until a toothpick inserted into the center comes out clean and the top is golden brown.
4. **Cool and Serve:**
   - Remove the cake from the oven and let it cool in the pan for about 10 minutes. Then, transfer it to a wire rack to cool completely.
   - Once cooled, slice and serve the Bolo de Noz. It can be enjoyed on its own or dusted with powdered sugar for decoration.

Tips:

- Make sure the walnuts are completely cooled before grinding to avoid them turning into walnut butter.
- For an extra layer of flavor, you can add a splash of port wine or brandy to the cake batter.
- Bolo de Noz is traditionally served at room temperature and pairs wonderfully with a cup of coffee or tea.

Enjoy making and savoring this delicious Portuguese Walnut Cake, celebrating its rich nutty taste and delightful texture!

Doce Fino (Portuguese Fine Pastry)

Ingredients:

For the Dough:

- 250g (about 2 cups) all-purpose flour
- 125g (about 1/2 cup) unsalted butter, softened
- 1 egg
- 50ml (about 1/4 cup) cold water
- Pinch of salt

For the Filling:

- 250g (about 1 1/4 cups) ground almonds
- 200g (about 1 cup) granulated sugar
- 2 large egg yolks
- Zest of 1 lemon
- 1/2 tsp ground cinnamon
- 1/4 tsp vanilla extract

For Assembly:

- Powdered sugar, for dusting

Instructions:

1. **Prepare the Dough:**
   - In a large mixing bowl, combine the flour and pinch of salt. Add the softened butter and rub it into the flour until the mixture resembles breadcrumbs.
   - Make a well in the center and add the egg. Gradually add the cold water while mixing with a fork or your hands, until the dough comes together. Form the dough into a ball, cover with plastic wrap, and refrigerate for 30 minutes.
2. **Make the Filling:**
   - In another bowl, combine the ground almonds, granulated sugar, lemon zest, ground cinnamon, and vanilla extract. Mix well.
   - Add the egg yolks to the almond mixture and mix until a thick paste forms. Set aside.
3. **Assemble the Doce Fino:**
   - Preheat your oven to 350°F (175°C). Line a baking sheet with parchment paper.
   - On a lightly floured surface, roll out the chilled dough into a thin rectangle, about 1/8 inch (3 mm) thick.
   - Spread the almond filling evenly over the rolled-out dough, leaving a small border around the edges.

- Carefully roll up the dough from one long side to form a log or cylinder. Gently transfer the log onto the prepared baking sheet, seam side down.
4. **Bake:**
    - Bake in the preheated oven for 25-30 minutes, or until the Doce Fino is golden brown and cooked through.
5. **Cool and Serve:**
    - Remove from the oven and let the Doce Fino cool on the baking sheet for 10 minutes. Then, transfer it to a wire rack to cool completely.
    - Once cooled, slice the Doce Fino into pieces. Dust with powdered sugar before serving.

Tips:

- The dough can be a bit delicate when rolling out, so work carefully to prevent tearing.
- You can experiment with different fillings such as coconut, chocolate, or fruit preserves for variations on Doce Fino.
- Store any leftovers in an airtight container at room temperature for a few days.

Enjoy making and savoring this classic Portuguese Fine Pastry, Doce Fino, with its almond-filled goodness and delicate pastry layers!

Biscoitos de Aguardente (Portuguese Brandy Biscuits)

Ingredients:

- 500g (about 4 cups) all-purpose flour
- 200g (about 1 cup) granulated sugar
- 150ml (about 2/3 cup) aguardente (Portuguese brandy)
- 150ml (about 2/3 cup) olive oil or vegetable oil
- Zest of 1 lemon
- 1 tsp baking powder
- Pinch of salt
- Granulated sugar, for rolling (optional)

Instructions:

1. **Mix the Dry Ingredients:**
   - In a large mixing bowl, combine the flour, granulated sugar, lemon zest, baking powder, and a pinch of salt. Mix well.
2. **Add the Wet Ingredients:**
   - Gradually add the aguardente and olive oil to the dry ingredients. Mix with a wooden spoon or your hands until a smooth dough forms. The dough should be soft and slightly sticky.
3. **Shape the Biscoitos:**
   - Preheat your oven to 350°F (175°C). Line a baking sheet with parchment paper.
   - Pinch off pieces of dough and roll them into small balls, about 1 inch (2.5 cm) in diameter. Place them on the prepared baking sheet, spacing them slightly apart.
4. **Bake:**
   - Bake in the preheated oven for 15-20 minutes, or until the Biscoitos are lightly golden brown.
5. **Optional Sugar Coating:**
   - While the Biscoitos are still warm, you can roll them in granulated sugar to coat them lightly, if desired.
6. **Cool and Serve:**
   - Transfer the Biscoitos de Aguardente to a wire rack to cool completely.
   - Once cooled, store them in an airtight container at room temperature.

Tips:

- Adjust the amount of aguardente to your preference. More aguardente will give the biscuits a stronger flavor.
- These biscuits are perfect with a cup of coffee or tea, or as a light snack.
- Biscoitos de Aguardente can be stored in an airtight container for several days, though they are best enjoyed fresh.

Enjoy making and savoring these delightful Portuguese Brandy Biscuits, Biscoitos de Aguardente, with their unique flavor and crispy texture!

Azevias de Batata Doce (Sweet Potato Turnovers)

Ingredients:

For the Dough:

- 500g (about 4 cups) all-purpose flour
- 100g (about 7 tbsp) unsalted butter, melted
- 1/2 tsp salt
- 1/2 cup warm water

For the Filling:

- 500g (about 1 lb) sweet potatoes (about 2 medium sweet potatoes)
- 100g (about 1/2 cup) granulated sugar (adjust to taste)
- Zest of 1 lemon
- 1/2 tsp ground cinnamon
- 1/4 tsp ground nutmeg
- 1/4 tsp ground cloves
- Pinch of salt

For Frying:

- Vegetable oil, for frying

For Serving:

- Powdered sugar, for dusting (optional)

Instructions:

1. **Prepare the Dough:**
   - In a large mixing bowl, combine the flour and salt. Make a well in the center and pour in the melted butter and warm water. Mix until the dough comes together. If needed, add a little more water, a tablespoon at a time, until the dough is smooth and elastic.
   - Cover the dough with a clean kitchen towel or plastic wrap and let it rest at room temperature while you prepare the filling.
2. **Prepare the Filling:**
   - Peel and chop the sweet potatoes into chunks. Place them in a saucepan and cover with water. Bring to a boil over medium-high heat, then reduce the heat and simmer until the sweet potatoes are tender, about 15-20 minutes.
   - Drain the sweet potatoes and mash them until smooth. Add the granulated sugar, lemon zest, ground cinnamon, ground nutmeg, ground cloves, and a pinch of

salt. Mix well until the filling is smooth and well combined. Adjust sweetness to your taste.
3. **Assemble the Azevias:**
    - On a lightly floured surface, roll out the dough thinly (about 1/8 inch or 3 mm thick). Use a round cookie cutter (about 3-4 inches or 7-10 cm in diameter) to cut out circles of dough.
    - Place a spoonful of the sweet potato filling in the center of each dough circle. Fold the dough over to form a half-moon shape and press the edges firmly to seal. You can use a fork to crimp the edges for a decorative touch.
4. **Fry the Azevias:**
    - In a large skillet or deep fryer, heat vegetable oil to 350°F (175°C).
    - Carefully place a few Azevias at a time into the hot oil, making sure not to overcrowd the pan. Fry until golden brown on both sides, about 2-3 minutes per side.
    - Remove the fried Azevias with a slotted spoon and drain on paper towels to remove excess oil.
5. **Serve:**
    - Once cooled slightly, dust the Azevias de Batata Doce with powdered sugar, if desired.
6. **Storage:**
    - Azevias can be stored in an airtight container at room temperature for a few days. They are best enjoyed fresh or lightly reheated.

Tips:

- Ensure the sweet potatoes are well mashed and seasoned for a smooth filling.
- Be cautious while frying to maintain an even golden color without burning the pastries.
- Azevias de Batata Doce are traditionally served during Christmas festivities but can be enjoyed throughout the year as a delicious sweet treat.

Enjoy making and savoring these traditional Portuguese Sweet Potato Turnovers, Azevias de Batata Doce, with their delightful sweet potato filling and crispy dough!

Bolo de Maçã (Portuguese Apple Cake)

Ingredients:

- 3 medium apples (such as Granny Smith or Gala)
- 200g (about 1 1/2 cups) all-purpose flour
- 150g (about 3/4 cup) granulated sugar
- 100ml (about 1/2 cup) milk
- 75g (about 1/3 cup) unsalted butter, melted and cooled
- 2 large eggs
- 1 tsp baking powder
- 1 tsp vanilla extract
- Zest of 1 lemon (optional)
- Pinch of salt

Instructions:

1. **Preheat the Oven:**
   - Preheat your oven to 350°F (175°C). Grease and flour a round cake pan (about 9 inches/23 cm in diameter).
2. **Prepare the Apples:**
   - Peel, core, and thinly slice the apples. Set aside.
3. **Mix the Dry Ingredients:**
   - In a large mixing bowl, whisk together the flour, baking powder, and a pinch of salt.
4. **Mix the Wet Ingredients:**
   - In another bowl, whisk together the eggs and granulated sugar until pale and fluffy. Add the melted butter, milk, vanilla extract, and lemon zest (if using). Mix until well combined.
5. **Combine Wet and Dry Ingredients:**
   - Gradually add the wet ingredients to the dry ingredients, stirring until just combined. Be careful not to overmix.
6. **Assemble the Cake:**
   - Pour half of the batter into the prepared cake pan and spread it evenly.
   - Arrange half of the apple slices on top of the batter in a single layer.
   - Pour the remaining batter over the apple slices and spread it gently to cover them.
   - Arrange the remaining apple slices on top in a decorative pattern.
7. **Bake:**
   - Bake in the preheated oven for 40-45 minutes, or until the cake is golden brown and a toothpick inserted into the center comes out clean.
8. **Cool and Serve:**
   - Allow the Bolo de Maçã to cool in the pan for about 10 minutes, then transfer it to a wire rack to cool completely.

- Slice and serve the cake at room temperature. Optionally, dust with powdered sugar before serving.

Tips:

- You can add a sprinkle of cinnamon or nutmeg to the batter for extra flavor.
- Adjust the amount of sugar depending on the sweetness of the apples and your preference.
- Bolo de Maçã is delicious served on its own or with a dollop of whipped cream or a scoop of vanilla ice cream.

Enjoy making and savoring this Portuguese Apple Cake, Bolo de Maçã, with its tender crumb and delicious apple flavor!

Pinhões (Portuguese Pine Nut Cookies)

Ingredients:

- 200g (about 1 1/2 cups) pine nuts
- 200g (about 1 1/2 cups) all-purpose flour
- 150g (about 3/4 cup) granulated sugar
- 100g (about 7 tbsp) unsalted butter, softened
- 1 large egg
- 1/2 tsp baking powder
- Pinch of salt
- Zest of 1 lemon (optional)

Instructions:

1. **Toast the Pine Nuts:**
   - Preheat your oven to 350°F (175°C). Spread the pine nuts evenly on a baking sheet and toast them in the oven for about 5-7 minutes, or until lightly golden and fragrant. Keep an eye on them as they can burn quickly. Remove from the oven and let them cool.
2. **Prepare the Dough:**
   - In a large mixing bowl, cream together the softened butter and granulated sugar until light and fluffy.
   - Add the egg and mix until well combined. Add the lemon zest if using.
   - In a separate bowl, whisk together the flour, baking powder, and a pinch of salt.
   - Gradually add the dry ingredients to the butter mixture, mixing until a dough forms.
3. **Shape the Cookies:**
   - Take portions of the dough and roll them into small balls, about 1 inch (2.5 cm) in diameter.
   - Roll each ball in the toasted pine nuts, pressing lightly so the nuts adhere to the dough.
   - Place the cookies on a baking sheet lined with parchment paper, spacing them slightly apart.
4. **Bake:**
   - Bake in the preheated oven for 12-15 minutes, or until the cookies are lightly golden brown.
5. **Cool and Serve:**
   - Remove the cookies from the oven and let them cool on the baking sheet for a few minutes.
   - Transfer the cookies to a wire rack to cool completely before serving.

Tips:

- Pine nuts can be quite expensive, so you can adjust the amount used based on your preference and budget.
- These cookies are delicate, so handle them gently when rolling and placing on the baking sheet.
- Store Pinhões in an airtight container at room temperature for several days. They can also be frozen for longer storage.

Enjoy making and savoring these traditional Portuguese Pine Nut Cookies, Pinhões, with their crunchy texture and nutty flavor!

Pão de Deus (Portuguese Bread of God)

Ingredients:

For the Dough:

- 500g (about 4 cups) all-purpose flour
- 100g (about 1/2 cup) granulated sugar
- 100ml (about 1/2 cup) milk
- 100ml (about 1/2 cup) water
- 75g (about 1/3 cup) unsalted butter, softened
- 2 large eggs
- 1 tsp instant yeast
- 1/2 tsp salt

For the Coconut Topping:

- 200g (about 2 cups) sweetened shredded coconut
- 100g (about 1/2 cup) granulated sugar
- 100ml (about 1/2 cup) milk
- 1 tbsp unsalted butter

For Glazing:

- 1 egg yolk
- 1 tbsp milk

Instructions:

1. **Prepare the Dough:**
   - In a small saucepan, heat the milk and water together until warm (not hot). Remove from heat and let it cool slightly.
   - In a large mixing bowl, combine the flour, sugar, instant yeast, and salt. Make a well in the center and add the softened butter and eggs.
   - Pour the warm milk and water mixture into the well. Mix everything together with a wooden spoon or your hands until a dough forms.
   - Knead the dough on a lightly floured surface for about 10 minutes, until smooth and elastic. Place the dough in a lightly greased bowl, cover with a clean kitchen towel or plastic wrap, and let it rise in a warm place for about 1-2 hours, or until doubled in size.
2. **Prepare the Coconut Topping:**
   - In a medium saucepan, combine the sweetened shredded coconut, granulated sugar, milk, and butter.
   - Cook over medium heat, stirring constantly, until the mixture thickens and comes together, about 5-7 minutes. Remove from heat and let it cool slightly.

3. **Shape and Assemble:**
   - Preheat your oven to 350°F (175°C). Line a baking sheet with parchment paper.
   - Punch down the risen dough and divide it into equal portions, about the size of a small bun (around 80g each). Shape each portion into a ball and place them on the prepared baking sheet, spacing them slightly apart.
   - Flatten each ball slightly with your hand. Spoon a generous amount of the coconut topping onto each flattened dough ball, spreading it out to cover the top.
4. **Glaze and Bake:**
   - In a small bowl, whisk together the egg yolk and milk for the glaze.
   - Brush the tops of the Pão de Deus with the egg yolk mixture.
   - Bake in the preheated oven for 15-20 minutes, or until the tops are golden brown and the bottoms are cooked through.
5. **Cool and Serve:**
   - Remove from the oven and let the Pão de Deus cool on a wire rack.
   - Serve warm or at room temperature. Enjoy these delightful Portuguese Bread of God as a sweet treat!

Tips:

- Make sure the coconut topping is thick enough to spread easily on top of the dough without running off.
- You can customize the sweetness of the coconut topping according to your preference.
- Pão de Deus is best enjoyed fresh on the day it is baked, but it can be stored in an airtight container at room temperature for a couple of days.

Enjoy making and savoring this traditional Portuguese sweet bread, Pão de Deus, with its delicious coconut topping!

Charutos de Ovos (Portuguese Egg Cigars)

Ingredients:

For the Filling:

- 8 egg yolks
- 200g (about 1 cup) granulated sugar
- Zest of 1 lemon
- Zest of 1 orange
- 1 cinnamon stick
- 100ml (about 1/2 cup) water

For the Dough:

- 250g (about 2 cups) all-purpose flour
- 100g (about 7 tbsp) unsalted butter, melted and cooled
- Pinch of salt
- 100ml (about 1/2 cup) water
- Vegetable oil, for frying

For Dusting:

- Powdered sugar, for dusting

Instructions:

1. **Prepare the Filling:**
   - In a saucepan, combine the sugar, lemon zest, orange zest, and cinnamon stick with the water. Bring to a boil over medium heat, stirring occasionally, until the sugar dissolves.
   - In a separate bowl, whisk the egg yolks. Slowly pour the hot sugar syrup into the egg yolks, whisking constantly to temper the yolks.
   - Return the mixture to the saucepan and cook over low heat, stirring constantly, until thickened and glossy (about 10-15 minutes). The consistency should be similar to custard.
   - Remove from heat and let it cool completely. Once cooled, remove the cinnamon stick.
2. **Prepare the Dough:**
   - In a large mixing bowl, combine the flour and a pinch of salt. Make a well in the center and pour in the melted butter and water. Mix until a smooth dough forms. If needed, add a little more water, a tablespoon at a time, until the dough is smooth and elastic.
   - Divide the dough into small portions and roll each portion into a thin circle or oval shape (about 3-4 inches/7-10 cm long and 2 inches/5 cm wide).

3. **Assemble the Charutos:**
   - Place a spoonful of the cooled egg yolk filling along one edge of each dough circle.
   - Fold the sides of the dough over the filling and roll it up tightly, resembling a cigar shape. Seal the edges by pressing them gently.
4. **Fry the Charutos:**
   - In a deep skillet or frying pan, heat vegetable oil over medium heat until hot (about 350°F/175°C).
   - Carefully place a few Charutos at a time into the hot oil, seam side down. Fry until golden brown and crispy on all sides, turning as needed.
   - Remove the fried Charutos with a slotted spoon and drain on paper towels to remove excess oil.
5. **Serve:**
   - Let the Charutos de Ovos cool slightly before dusting them generously with powdered sugar.
   - Serve warm or at room temperature. They are best enjoyed fresh!

Tips:

- Be cautious while frying to maintain an even golden color without burning the Charutos.
- You can adjust the amount of sugar in the filling according to your preference.
- Store any leftover Charutos de Ovos in an airtight container at room temperature for up to a few days.

Enjoy making and savoring these delightful Portuguese Egg Cigars, Charutos de Ovos, with their sweet, custardy filling and crispy exterior!

Pão de Rala (Portuguese Bread of Rala)

Ingredients:

For the Dough:

- 500g (about 4 cups) cornbread crumbs (preferably from cornbread made with corn flour, known as "milho")
- 250g (about 1 1/4 cups) granulated sugar
- 250g (about 2 1/4 cups) ground almonds
- 8 large egg yolks
- Zest of 1 lemon
- Zest of 1 orange
- 1 tbsp ground cinnamon
- 1/2 tsp ground cloves
- 1/2 tsp ground nutmeg
- 100ml (about 1/2 cup) aguardente (Portuguese brandy)
- 100ml (about 1/2 cup) olive oil

For Garnish:

- Ground cinnamon, for dusting

Instructions:

1. **Prepare the Dough:**
    - In a large mixing bowl, combine the cornbread crumbs, granulated sugar, ground almonds, lemon zest, orange zest, ground cinnamon, ground cloves, and ground nutmeg. Mix well.
    - Make a well in the center of the dry ingredients and add the egg yolks, aguardente, and olive oil.
    - Mix everything together until well combined. The dough should be sticky and hold together when pressed.
2. **Shape and Bake:**
    - Preheat your oven to 350°F (175°C). Line a baking sheet with parchment paper.
    - Divide the dough into portions and shape each portion into round or oval loaves, about 3-4 inches (7-10 cm) in diameter and 1 inch (2.5 cm) thick.
    - Place the loaves on the prepared baking sheet, leaving some space between them.
3. **Bake:**
    - Bake in the preheated oven for 25-30 minutes, or until the Pão de Rala is lightly golden brown on top and cooked through. The edges may crack slightly, which is normal.
4. **Cool and Serve:**

- Remove from the oven and let the Pão de Rala cool on the baking sheet for a few minutes.
- Transfer to a wire rack to cool completely.

5. **Serve:**
   - Once cooled, dust the tops of the Pão de Rala with ground cinnamon.
   - Slice and serve at room temperature. Enjoy this traditional Portuguese dessert with a cup of coffee or tea!

Tips:

- Cornbread crumbs are essential for the texture and flavor of Pão de Rala. You can make them by crumbling cornbread made with corn flour (not cornmeal).
- Adjust the sweetness and spice levels to your preference.
- Store Pão de Rala in an airtight container at room temperature for several days. It can also be frozen for longer storage.

Enjoy making and savoring this special Portuguese dessert, Pão de Rala, with its rich almond flavor and aromatic spices!

Bolo de Cenoura (Portuguese Carrot Cake)

Ingredients:

For the Cake:

- 3 large carrots (about 300g), peeled and grated
- 3 large eggs, at room temperature
- 200ml (about 1 cup) vegetable oil
- 250g (about 1 1/4 cups) granulated sugar
- 250g (about 2 cups) all-purpose flour
- 1 tsp baking powder
- 1/2 tsp baking soda
- 1/2 tsp ground cinnamon
- Pinch of salt

For the Chocolate Glaze:

- 100g (about 1/2 cup) dark chocolate, chopped
- 50g (about 1/4 cup) unsalted butter
- 2 tbsp milk
- 2 tbsp granulated sugar (optional, for a sweeter glaze)

Instructions:

1. **Preheat the Oven:**
   - Preheat your oven to 350°F (175°C). Grease and flour a round cake pan (about 9 inches/23 cm in diameter).
2. **Prepare the Cake:**
   - In a large mixing bowl, whisk together the vegetable oil and granulated sugar until well combined.
   - Add the eggs one at a time, mixing well after each addition.
   - Stir in the grated carrots until evenly distributed.
   - In a separate bowl, sift together the flour, baking powder, baking soda, ground cinnamon, and a pinch of salt.
   - Gradually add the dry ingredients to the wet ingredients, mixing until just combined. Be careful not to overmix.
3. **Bake the Cake:**
   - Pour the batter into the prepared cake pan and spread it evenly.
   - Bake in the preheated oven for 30-35 minutes, or until a toothpick inserted into the center comes out clean.
4. **Make the Chocolate Glaze:**
   - While the cake is baking, prepare the chocolate glaze. In a heatproof bowl set over a pot of simmering water (double boiler method), melt the chopped dark chocolate and unsalted butter, stirring occasionally until smooth.

- Stir in the milk and granulated sugar (if using), mixing until the sugar dissolves and the glaze is smooth and glossy. Remove from heat and set aside to cool slightly.

5. **Glaze the Cake:**
   - Once the cake is baked and cooled for about 10 minutes in the pan, carefully remove it from the pan and transfer it to a wire rack to cool completely.
   - Pour the chocolate glaze over the cooled cake, spreading it evenly with a spatula or knife. Allow the glaze to set before slicing and serving.
6. **Serve:**
   - Slice and serve the Bolo de Cenoura at room temperature.

Tips:

- You can add chopped nuts (such as walnuts or pecans) to the cake batter for added texture and flavor.
- Adjust the sweetness of the glaze by adding more or less sugar according to your taste.
- Store any leftover cake in an airtight container at room temperature for a few days, or refrigerate for longer storage.

Enjoy making and savoring this delicious Portuguese Carrot Cake, Bolo de Cenoura, with its moist crumb and rich chocolate glaze!

Pastel de Chaves (Chaves Pastry)

Ingredients:

For the Dough:

- 500g (about 4 cups) all-purpose flour
- 100g (about 7 tbsp) unsalted butter, cold and cut into cubes
- 1 tsp salt
- 150ml (about 2/3 cup) cold water

For the Filling:

- 300g (about 10.5 oz) ground beef or pork (or a combination)
- 1 onion, finely chopped
- 2 cloves of garlic, minced
- 1/2 red bell pepper, finely chopped
- 1 tbsp tomato paste
- 1 tbsp olive oil
- 1/2 tsp ground cumin
- 1/2 tsp paprika
- Salt and pepper, to taste
- Chopped fresh parsley, for garnish (optional)

For Assembly:

- 1 egg yolk, beaten (for egg wash)
- Olive oil or butter, for brushing

Instructions:

1. **Prepare the Dough:**
   - In a large mixing bowl, combine the flour and salt. Add the cold butter cubes and rub them into the flour mixture using your fingertips, until it resembles coarse breadcrumbs.
   - Gradually add the cold water, mixing with a fork or your hands until the dough comes together. Be careful not to overwork the dough. Shape it into a ball, wrap in plastic wrap, and refrigerate for at least 30 minutes.
2. **Prepare the Filling:**
   - Heat olive oil in a large skillet over medium heat. Add the chopped onion and cook until softened, about 3-4 minutes.
   - Add the minced garlic and cook for another minute until fragrant.
   - Add the ground beef or pork to the skillet, breaking it up with a spoon. Cook until browned and cooked through, stirring occasionally.

- Stir in the chopped bell pepper, tomato paste, ground cumin, paprika, salt, and pepper. Cook for another 5-7 minutes, or until the mixture is well combined and any excess liquid has evaporated. Remove from heat and let it cool slightly.

3. **Assemble the Pastel de Chaves:**
   - Preheat your oven to 375°F (190°C). Line a baking sheet with parchment paper.
   - On a lightly floured surface, roll out the chilled dough to a thickness of about 1/8 inch (3 mm). Using a round cutter (about 4-5 inches/10-12 cm in diameter), cut out circles of dough.
   - Place a spoonful of the cooled meat filling in the center of each dough circle. Fold the dough over to form a half-moon shape, pressing the edges firmly to seal. You can crimp the edges with a fork for a decorative finish.
   - Place the pastries on the prepared baking sheet. Brush the tops with beaten egg yolk for a golden finish.

4. **Bake the Pastel de Chaves:**
   - Bake in the preheated oven for 20-25 minutes, or until the pastries are golden brown and cooked through.

5. **Serve:**
   - Remove from the oven and let the Pastel de Chaves cool slightly on a wire rack.
   - Optionally, brush the tops with a little olive oil or melted butter for extra shine. Garnish with chopped parsley if desired.
   - Serve warm or at room temperature. Pastel de Chaves makes a delicious snack or appetizer.

Tips:

- You can make the filling ahead of time and refrigerate it until ready to use.
- Feel free to customize the filling with additional spices or herbs according to your taste.
- Pastel de Chaves can be stored in an airtight container in the refrigerator for a few days. Reheat in the oven before serving to crisp up the pastry.

Enjoy making and savoring this authentic Portuguese savory pastry, Pastel de Chaves, filled with deliciously spiced meat!

Castanhas de Ovos (Portuguese Chestnuts of Eggs)

Ingredients:

- 12 egg yolks
- 300g (about 1 1/2 cups) granulated sugar
- 150ml (about 2/3 cup) water
- 1 tbsp lemon juice
- 1 tbsp unsalted butter, softened
- Ground cinnamon, for dusting (optional)

Instructions:

1. **Prepare the Syrup:**
   - In a small saucepan, combine the granulated sugar and water over medium heat, stirring until the sugar dissolves.
   - Add the lemon juice to the sugar syrup. Bring the mixture to a boil and then reduce the heat to low. Let it simmer for about 5-7 minutes until it reaches a syrupy consistency (about 220°F/105°C on a candy thermometer). Remove from heat and set aside.
2. **Prepare the Egg Yolk Mixture:**
   - In a large mixing bowl, whisk the egg yolks until smooth and creamy.
   - Gradually pour the hot sugar syrup into the egg yolks, whisking constantly to temper the yolks and prevent them from curdling.
3. **Cook the Mixture:**
   - Transfer the mixture back into the saucepan and place it over low heat. Stir continuously with a wooden spoon or silicone spatula until the mixture thickens and starts to pull away from the sides of the pan. This will take about 15-20 minutes.
   - Add the softened butter and continue stirring until well combined and the mixture has a smooth consistency.
4. **Shape and Serve:**
   - Remove the mixture from heat and let it cool slightly until it's comfortable to handle.
   - With buttered hands, shape the mixture into small chestnut-sized balls or shape them into small mounds using a spoon.
   - Optionally, dust the Castanhas de Ovos with ground cinnamon for extra flavor and decoration.
5. **Storage:**
   - Allow the Castanhas de Ovos to cool completely before serving. Store any leftovers in an airtight container in the refrigerator for up to a week.

Tips:

- Work quickly when shaping the Castanhas de Ovos, as the mixture can become sticky as it cools.
- You can customize the flavor by adding a dash of vanilla extract or a sprinkle of ground cinnamon to the egg yolk mixture.
- These sweet egg fudge balls are typically enjoyed as a dessert or snack, often served during festive occasions in Portugal.

Enjoy making and savoring this delightful Portuguese dessert, Castanhas de Ovos, with its rich, sweet egg flavor!

Coscorões (Portuguese Fried Pastry)

Ingredients:

- 500g (about 4 cups) all-purpose flour
- 4 large eggs
- 50g (about 1/4 cup) unsalted butter, melted
- 100ml (about 1/2 cup) milk
- 50g (about 1/4 cup) granulated sugar
- Zest of 1 lemon
- Pinch of salt
- Vegetable oil, for frying
- Powdered sugar or cinnamon sugar, for dusting

Instructions:

1. **Prepare the Dough:**
   - In a large mixing bowl, combine the flour, granulated sugar, and pinch of salt.
   - Make a well in the center and add the eggs, melted butter, milk, and lemon zest.
   - Mix everything together until a dough forms. Knead the dough on a lightly floured surface for about 5-7 minutes until smooth and elastic. If the dough is too sticky, add a little more flour as needed.
   - Cover the dough with a clean kitchen towel and let it rest for about 30 minutes.
2. **Roll and Cut the Dough:**
   - On a lightly floured surface, roll out the dough to a thickness of about 1/4 inch (0.5 cm).
   - Use a sharp knife or a pastry cutter to cut the dough into strips or diamond shapes, about 4-5 inches (10-12 cm) long and 1 inch (2.5 cm) wide.
3. **Fry the Coscorões:**
   - In a deep skillet or frying pan, heat vegetable oil over medium heat until it reaches about 350°F (175°C).
   - Carefully place a few pieces of dough into the hot oil, frying them in batches without overcrowding the pan. Fry for about 2-3 minutes on each side, or until golden brown and crispy.
   - Use a slotted spoon or tongs to remove the fried Coscorões and place them on a plate lined with paper towels to absorb excess oil.
4. **Serve:**
   - While still warm, dust the Coscorões generously with powdered sugar or cinnamon sugar.
   - Serve immediately as a delicious snack or dessert.

Tips:

- The dough can also be rolled out and cut into different shapes like circles or rectangles.

- Make sure the oil is hot enough before frying to ensure the Coscorões cook evenly and become crispy.
- Store any leftover Coscorões in an airtight container at room temperature. Reheat briefly in the oven before serving to restore crispiness.

Enjoy making and savoring these crispy Portuguese Coscorões, perfect for festive occasions or any time you crave a delightful fried pastry!

Pão de Ló de Alfeizerão (Alfeizerão Sponge Cake)

Ingredients:

- 6 large eggs, at room temperature
- 200g (about 1 cup) granulated sugar
- 100g (about 1 cup) finely ground almonds (almond flour)
- 50g (about 1/3 cup) all-purpose flour
- Zest of 1 lemon
- 1/2 tsp baking powder
- Pinch of salt

Instructions:

1. **Preheat the Oven:**
   - Preheat your oven to 350°F (175°C). Grease and line a round cake pan (about 9 inches/23 cm in diameter) with parchment paper.
2. **Prepare the Batter:**
   - In a large mixing bowl, beat the eggs and sugar together with an electric mixer until pale and fluffy, about 5-7 minutes.
   - Add the lemon zest and continue beating until well incorporated.
   - In a separate bowl, sift together the almond flour, all-purpose flour, baking powder, and a pinch of salt.
   - Gradually fold the dry ingredients into the egg mixture using a spatula, being careful not to deflate the batter.
3. **Bake the Cake:**
   - Pour the batter into the prepared cake pan and smooth the top with a spatula.
   - Bake in the preheated oven for 25-30 minutes, or until the cake is golden brown on top and a toothpick inserted into the center comes out clean.
4. **Cool and Serve:**
   - Remove the cake from the oven and let it cool in the pan for about 10 minutes.
   - Carefully transfer the cake to a wire rack to cool completely.
5. **Serve:**
   - Once cooled, slice and serve the Pão de Ló de Alfeizerão. It is delicious on its own or with a dusting of powdered sugar.

Tips:

- Make sure the eggs are at room temperature for better volume when beating with sugar.
- Folding the dry ingredients gently into the batter helps maintain the cake's light and airy texture.
- Store any leftover cake in an airtight container at room temperature for up to a few days.

Enjoy making and savoring this delightful Portuguese sponge cake, Pão de Ló de Alfeizerão, with its delicate almond flavor and tender crumb!